SYDNEY'S BLEU

JOURNEY OF A GIRL WHO NEVER GAVE UP ON LOVE

ALICIA HILAIRE

Susan, I appreciate you & I'm so glad we met. I'm wishing you much success, peace and happiness! May God continue to Bless You

Copyright © 2019 Hilaire Wellness & Beauty Clinics INC

All rights reserved. No part of this publication may be reproduced, distributed, or transmitted in any way form or by any means, including photocopying, recording, or other electronic or mechanical methods, without the prior permission of the publisher, except in the case of brief quotations invited in critical reviews and certain other noncommercial uses permitted by copyright law. For permission requests, write to the publisher addressed "attention permission coordinator" at the address below.

Copyright cover art images and use licenses were secured through

Shutterstock and 123rf.

Portions of this book are works of non-fiction. Certain names and identifying characteristics have been used or changed as appropriate.

Some portions of this book are works of fiction. Any reference to historical events, real people, or real places are used fictitiously. Other names, characters, places, and events are products of the author's imagination, and any resemblances to actual events or places or persons living, or dead are entirely coincidental.

ISBN 978-0-578-62396-2 (paperback)

Library of Congress control number: TXu 2-175-814

Hilaire, Alicia. Sydney's Bleu. – 1st ed.

Publisher: Hilaire Wellness & Beauty Clinics INC

Editor: Kelly Cook

Illustration, design, cover design, titles by Garrett Cook & Kelly Cook

Book printing By Alpha Graphics, Suwanee, Georgia

www.us717.alphagraphics.com

Dedicated To:

Alexis and Rolande

Contents

Foreword i

Preface iii

Acknowledgments vii

    Chapter 1: Family Ties... 1

    Chapter 2: Splashing in Holy Water 15

    Chapter 3: Sydney's Baggage 27

    Chapter 4: Me Too 41

    Chapter 5: Teenage Drama 49

    Chapter 6: Love and War with a Muslim 67

    Chapter 7: Riding Dirty... 77

    Chapter 8: Dreams of Death 91

    Chapter 9: Lust and Deception 99

    Chapter 10: Rollercoaster Gone Bad 117

    Chapter 11: Europe Bound................................ 143

    Chapter 12: Haiti 201

Foreword

The idea of writing this book came over twenty years ago. I felt inspired to write about some of the tragedies that I had faced. The purpose of finally releasing the words in this book is two-fold. I hope this book will help women who are coping with life's issues, and I hope by sharing my story, women will begin to heal. It is evident that women grow, develop, and sometimes gain courage by sharing their stories.

As I faced battle after battle, I felt defeated continuously, and, in my mind, I thought that my battle wounds were a sign of complete failure. Over the years, I felt worthless as I suffered in silence. I couldn't tell anyone about the internal battle, dealing with what doctors call "major depression." The negativity associated with mental illness was a topic that I preferred to keep in the closet.

In this book, there are some traumatic stories, poems, and, hopefully, some inspiration. The journey of

Sydney Marie begins in Saginaw, Michigan, and will take detours through several remote places on earth.

Preface

The stories that follow are inspired by actual events that have helped to shape my life. Writing these stories about various experiences has given me a better understanding of who I am as a person. This book does not define who I am, nor does it explain what God has in store for me. I wrote this book of short stories to help with the healing process and to help others persevere throughout this journey called life. I have changed some of the names and changed some of the settings in the stories to protect my family and loved ones. The stories are small pieces of a puzzle that, in the end, will be glued together and hopefully make sense to my family and my children. If this book can help one young woman or one person realize their true potential, I will have succeeded in my mission to leave this world a little bit better.

Dreams, childhood experiences, family, and friends have all contributed to this collection. The wrong choices and unhealthy relationships shared in this book were challenges that I had to overcome. Still, they also provided the opportunity to learn life lessons. Shared here are stories of situations, revealed to allow the readers to know that we're all real people who have experienced situations that sometimes occur in life. My hope and dreams are that my children can learn from my mistakes. I want them to look at my life as an example and choose to do what's right. I also want them to recognize that there will be consequences for their actions. Doing good will generally present a good outcome and doing what's wrong will cause you so much pain and unnecessary disappointment. To the women that read this book, please read it with a strong understanding that if you don't set high standards for yourself, no one else will. I encourage you to save your heart and your body for serving God. When you give your heart and body to another person, you have given away your power, and you have given away what's most sacred to God.

    When you're out in the world and choose to give your heart away, you open yourself to other people's spirits. You will find yourself expecting more from people than what they are capable of giving or expecting to see yourself reflected in others; this is when disappointment sets in. You will hope, wish, and pray that other people feel the same way as you, but they won't.

These words come from experience and knowledge gained through stories told to me and through my trials and errors. Each time you open your heart and allow someone into your bed, after the physical act runs its course, there is a feeling of emptiness.

Personally, I had an unfulfilled expectation that the person would love me because my heart was always in it. As women, sometimes we allow intimacy after a brief courtship, several movie dates, and dinner. Then genuinely hope and pray that the man of the moment would fall in love and be your happily ever after. That dream rarely ever happens; therefore, the usual outcome is disappointment every time. We repeatedly give our time, our heart, and our body but are left with nothing. The men rarely ever stay around, resulting in relationships usually lasting for two or possibly three months. Men will keep turning left and right through the revolving door of your heart if you allow it.

Later in life, I learned some valuable lessons: Your first love should always be God. Your second love should be love for yourself. Your third love should be love for your family and friends. Take good care of yourself. Love yourself like there is no tomorrow. Exercise your mind. Knowledge truly is power. Be the best version of you that you can be and enjoy this life while you are here because tomorrow is not guaranteed. As I write these things, I am speaking to you, but most importantly, I am encouraging myself.

Acknowledgments

First and foremost, I thank God for calling me out of the deep darkness that once encapsulated my entire existence. Thank you for giving me the courage to tell my story. I have been in constant communication with my creator about my ministry; all glory is given to the Heavenly Father, amen. I thank my family for their ongoing support and understanding. Thank you for allowing me the time I needed to complete this assignment. Thanks to my parents for all that you've done, especially Mom.

Most importantly, I want to express my love for my beautiful children DeJuan, Bryce, Breyel, Jasmine, and Andre. You all are my inspiration and precious gifts from God. I love you all dearly. Bill Moore, thank you so much for always encouraging me to tell my story. Mr. Taylor, thank you for always treating me with kindness and respect. Thank you for being a positive role model and a great father to the little people. Max, I appreciate you, and I thank you for being a friend and always believing in me. Thank you for giving me a place to stay when I needed time to think about life and write this story. Sis, thanks for always being real with me on the spiritual level. You are a true friend. I am so glad that you are my sister. Believing in the power of God and giving me the uplifting talks has empowered me to serve God better.

    Ralph and Ramon, I am thankful to have you as my brothers; you guys made me tough. Grandma Nadine, thank you for allowing me to get baptized when I was a child. In my heart, I will always believe that God kept me safe and protected my life because you cared enough about us to send that church bus to pick us up on Sunday mornings. Because of you, I know God. Thank you to my exes. Even though there was a lot of hurt and pain, I am thankful for the lessons learned. I am thankful that God allowed me to exchange ideas and share my love. I am grateful for the unique experiences, which helped me to determine what type of woman I would become. I sincerely thank you. A special thanks to the women who critiqued the first draft: Vanessa Madden, Kelly Cook, Wanda Hall, Zelda Millner, Mrs. Zhao, Alexis Bond, Andrea Stroman, and Lisa Godwin. Thanks

Acknowledgments

to my forever friends, you've been by my side through the storms and back. With love and respect, I sincerely thank you.

Lastly, and most importantly, to my amazing husband, Frantz, you are the most talented and brilliant man that I have ever met. You have been a steadfast positive role model to all our family and friends. You are the best, and I love you for accepting me as I am. Your love, support, friendship, and encouragement throughout the years have meant so much to me. Thank you for standing by my side through the good times and all the time. I love who you are and what you stand for. May God continue to bless us!

SYDNEY'S BLEU

Chapter 1: Family Ties

A Letter from Sydney:

Hello, my name is Sydney-Ann Marie; friends and family usually just refer to me as Syd. In my natural and physical state of being the world recognizes me as Sydney, the loner, or Syd, the girl who consistently has something stupid to say or says nothing at all. My personality is typically misunderstood and frowned upon because I'm not as normal as ordinary people are supposed to be. I've been laughed at and teased because of my dark-brown skin complexion inherited from my African ancestors. I'm referred to as "weird" because I over-analyze everything, which causes a delayed response as I talk slowly and drag my words. I've been called many terrible names like Buckwheat, Kunta Kinte, Blacky, Black-Dog, and more derogatory terms like bit** and whore. Being called bad names doesn't hurt, but the thoughts of the meaning behind those words has had a horrific effect on my life.

Standing in the depth of my inner-self, and in my supernatural existence, is a God-fearing child. This child is trying to transition from the pits and pains of the past to a land where there's breathable air that flows through the lungs and is exhaled out of the mouth. My inner-self longs for pure love and acceptance. I long for something that I do not have courage enough to give to myself. Sometimes I sincerely dislike Sydney, and she's not so fond of me; therefore, my inner-self and outer-self are in constant conflict. The conflict is like an inner battle between good and evil or an inner child and outer adult. My internal dichotomy is so extreme at times that I often refer to them separately or collectively.

Slowly, I've come to the realization that I am Sydney, and unfortunately, she resides within me. We are still together because her attempt to end our life failed. You see, Sydney swallowed a bottle of pain killers, drank half a bottle of Vodka, and chugged down a bottle of liquid cold medication as a suicide attempt. That night was the first time that I realized my internal conflict and didn't want any association with someone, so repulsive. Sydney didn't deserve to live, but I, the levelheaded self, stayed up all night and prayed to my Heavenly Father and asked Him to forgive Sydney and give her another chance. I pleaded with God and begged him to protect Sydney. If someone commits suicide, they are probably securing their position in hell, so I implored God, "Please God, we need you. Please God enter this place and save Sydney from the eternal fire of hell".

August 16th, 1977, at three o'clock in the afternoon, Elvis Presley was pronounced dead. At the exact same moment, doctors at Saginaw General

Chapter 1: Family Ties

Hospital were pulling my head from my mother's womb. Grandma Nadeya always told me that I was special, but I never understood why "God took Elvis home to make room for you, Sydney… Wade in the water…" Grandma Nadeya would say.

My bloodline and family history have always been with me regardless of my many attempts to break away from the negativity and misunderstanding associated with our secretly dysfunctional genes. I'll never forget the day that my mom told me about our father. "Sydney," she said, "your father's DNA contains many mental disorders, such as paranoia, anxiety, and schizophrenia." She went on to tell me (and my inner child Sydney) that she and Daddy started dating back in nineteen sixty-five. "Your dad and I had been together since I was twelve years old. After graduating from Saginaw High School in nineteen seventy-one, we got married when we were both only eighteen years old. I gave your daddy an ultimatum; he had to marry me, or I wouldn't wait for him, and if he didn't marry me, I would move on with my life." My mom said that before she and our father married and he went off to join the

United States Air Force, he left Saginaw as a normal, mentally healthy man.

    Our father completed eight weeks of basic training at Lackland Air Force Base in San Antonio, Texas. Mom explained, "While your dad was there in basic training, he made collect calls to me every chance he got. I accepted all of your dad's collect calls because I would receive a monthly wife allowance, or an allotment provided to me by the government".

    After completing basic training, Dad was stationed at Chanute Air Force Base in Rantoul, Illinois. In love and anxious to become an adult, Mom moved to Rantoul to be with Dad. They lived in a barely furnished one-bedroom apartment off base for a few months while Dad was there to do his technical training. Mom couldn't remember what Dad's job was, but she did recall how handsome dad looked in his fitted Air Force uniform.

    After Dad completed his training in Rantoul, he then was stationed at Wright Patterson Air Force Base in Dayton, Ohio. Mom explained, "Your daddy never went to fight in a war. During military service, he was admitted to Wright VA Hospital after he had complained to one of the Air Force lieutenants about hearing voices in his head. Your father said the voices wouldn't go away, so the Air Force transported him to Wright VA Hospital so that he could get a psychological evaluation."

    During his first visit to Wright VA Hospital, the doctors administered several lab tests, which included: blood work, a urine test, and a brain scan. Dad also had to undergo multiple verbal and written questionnaires to categorize the symptoms that he was experiencing. A few days later, after acknowledging there was no trace of alcohol or drugs in his system, the psychiatrists had diagnosed Dad with acute schizophrenia.

    Mom said that she went to visit Dad while he was in the VA hospital. Mom described his behavior as abnormal. She said, "Your father was on a lot of antipsychotic medication, he sauntered like a soulless corpse, and his speech pattern was slurred and distorted." Mom couldn't explain what had happened to Dad, but she insisted that he was not the same man that she had married a year ago. Mom couldn't recognize the man that she had once loved. A few months later, the United

States Air Force discharged Dad from the military and sent him back home to return as a disabled civilian in Saginaw, Michigan.

AIRMANSHIP AND CORE VALUES

MISSION: Transform civilians into motivated, disciplined warrior Airmen with the foundation to serve in the world's greatest Air Force.

VISION: Develop the next generation of Airmen who embody absolute professionalism!

Before becoming an Airman, Dad had to be in some sort of good health to pass the physical medical exam required to enlist in the Air Force. He also had to be kind of smart to meet the specific scoring requirements to pass the written tests given on the ASVAB. Mom explained in disbelief, "Sydney, something strange happened in the military, and whatever happened while your father was there contributed to ruining his life." What is a child to do

Chapter 1: Family Ties

with this information? Me and my inner self struggled to sort things out. Dad didn't have acute schizophrenia before signing up for the military; why would the Air Force agree to enlist someone that was psychologically unstable? Whatever happened to dad during his time in the Air Force remains a mystery.

After being discharged from the military, Dad came back to reunite with his family in Saginaw. Dad was never psychologically the same; his cognitive abilities had diminished. His diagnosis of acute schizophrenia morphed into extreme paranoia; he thought everybody was watching him and following him. Dad habitually accused Mom of cheating on him. He didn't trust anyone, and he was repeatedly admitted into the VA hospital in Battle Creek, Michigan.

Our mother, Felicia, also known as *Miss Brickhouse,* was drop-dead gorgeous. Her sun-kissed bronze skin, huge light-brown eyes, sharp facial bone structure, and long black hair implied that she was of Western Indian descent. She glowed like a goddess, yet her genetic makeup contained an ounce of low self-worth and shattered self-esteem seemingly passed down from early generations of field slaves. Despite the darkness of her past hurts, she had a substantial amount of determination and enough love to heal an entire nation.

The only toxic waste in Mom's bloodline was the love of money and the will to get it by any means necessary. She would primarily engage in consensual transactions, which usually involved two components: a man and money. Her mother, our grandmother, Marie, loved men, and she too, loved money. Marie only had a second-grade education when she chose to drop out of school. Mom shared with us, "Marie had to work in the fields of Arkansas, picking cotton instead of getting an education." Mom went on to explain, "Marie's skin was so light that she could pass as a Caucasian woman. Marie was also beautiful. She was a flapper; she used to sing and dance in nightclubs as a young lady. She had many partners, and four different men fathered all four of her daughters."

All of Marie's daughters thoroughly enjoyed the nightlife! Well, let me clarify, Felicia was not actually a lady of the night. Still, she stayed with our father because he was the sole provider for his family, and he bought our mother everything that you could imagine. Dad laced mom with material things from furs, cars, and houses to expensive jewelry. Dad even managed to purchase Mom the most substantial home in our neighborhood. Dad struggled to give Mom everything she asked for.

As a child, I watched and observed everything our parents did. Yes, that means Sydney did as well. I promised never to do some of the things we saw our parents do, but then there were a few things that I could not control. Our father taught us so many valuable lessons, both good and bad. The good that we learned from our father was to be an excellent provider for our family.

Although Daddy suffered from several addictions, including alcoholism, prescription drugs, street drugs, gambling, and women, he managed to work a regular nine to five job. Daddy worked as a supervisor at the *Trinity Community Center*, then after he finished up at work, he hustled. He rolled dice in the local gambling houses throughout Saginaw, and he regularly bet on horses at the racetrack. Daddy was the pimp of many women, and he sold drugs.

By watching our father in action, Syd and I learned the effects and damages caused by using or engaging in drugs. The result of watching Daddy get strung out on cocaine made my whole being too afraid to use drugs. I was obsessively scared to use drugs. Still, I wasn't afraid to deliver a five-dollar bag of greenery to some of my friends every now and then.

Some of our father's side of the family were associated with the local hustlers and drug pushers of Saginaw. Back in the early nineteen eighties, two of our uncles were caught up in the line of fire while hanging out with their drug-dealing friend, Sam. Uncle George and Uncle Winston were not drug dealers; they were tenured employees at General Motors. Unfortunately, during a drug-related shooting, Dad's youngest brother, Uncle Winston, was shot twenty-two times. Dad's oldest brother, Uncle George, was shot seven times. Of course, Dad's youngest brother, Uncle Winston, didn't survive. Dad's oldest brother, Uncle George, did survive the shooting, but he was paralyzed for life. The seven

Chapter 1: Family Ties

gunshot bullets fractured both of his legs and his spine. The doctors had to amputate both of Uncle George's legs and reconstruct his sacrum and lower lumbar for him to live. This drug-related incident drove our father into a deep depression, on top of the fact that he was already suffering from other mental disorders.

    Shortly after the traumatic shooting of Uncle Winston and Uncle George, Daddy began to smoke crack-rocks and snort cocaine. First, a dealer, then a user; Daddy had become his own best client. Drug use was Daddy's way of coping with the uncertainties that street-life can bring. He needed a way out, and the drugs allowed him to, momentarily, escape the streets that haunted his fragile existence. Watching Daddy abuse drugs made me know for sure that I didn't want to go down that route.

    When Daddy was high, he would trip so hard; it was like he was a possessed zombie. When he was high on cocaine, his eyes would turn red and make him look like a demonic villain. Whenever he came home, high on drugs, he would force me to climb into the attic with a flashlight to search for money and gold. While high on drugs, Dad was convinced that the previous owners of our home were millionaires and that they had left a treasure chest with silver, gold, and a fortune in the attic. I would stay in the attic for hours "looking for money," but I would doze off while up there and sometimes ignore Daddy's request altogether. If I tried to come down from the attic, Daddy would make me go back up and search some more. This routine had become a regular part of my life for at least two years of my childhood.

As a child, I can recall watching Daddy have sex in a hotel with some strange looking woman that was not our mother. I remember walking up the stairs of an orange and white hotel building on East Genesis Street in Saginaw, Michigan. I also remember the hotel room had two beds. Daddy and the strange-looking lady were on one bed, and I was on the other bed. (Me and my inner self Sydney that is….)

Daddy gently demanded, "Sydney, lay over there on that other bed. Close your eyes and turn your face towards the opposite wall. Just go to sleep and don't look over here." I was obedient, so I looked away from

Chapter 1: Family Ties

Daddy and the strange woman. But I heard every moan and groan too wild animals could make. I was just a kid; I was so confused. I hated what happened in that hotel room, but I loved Daddy so much that I wouldn't dare tell our mother about the incident.

From that day on, subconsciously, I festered deep hatred toward all women. I promised that I would never trust women ever again. I also lost all respect for our mother. I was mad at Mom because I believed Mom probably did something terrible to make our dad hangout with that woman in the hotel. Me and my inner person both didn't get it. We both were totally confused. What a horrible experience for an innocent five-year-old child to endure and what a gruesome hidden scar it left on me. That traumatic incident, along with the confusion it presented, coupled with genetic DNA that carries a history of mental illness, has burdened my soul for quite some time.

SYDNEY'S BLEU

Chapter 2: Splashing in Holy Water

ঠ 2 ঠ

Chapter 2: Splashing in Holy Water

The rusted old white church bus traveled through the deserted streets of Saginaw to pick us up at eight o'clock a.m. on Sunday mornings. Grandma Nadeya knew that our household was in turmoil, so she had arranged for one of the deacons from her church to make a special bus pickup at our address, located at twenty-one Delray Street, where my siblings and I resided with our parents. I can't recall my parents ever going to church, yet if they did, it was only on a rare occasion like Easter Sunday. That didn't stop Grandma Nadeya from trying to protect her grandchildren from the bad decisions our parents made. Grandma Nadeya was fully committed to the duty of making sure we knew the Lord.

Every Sunday morning, my brothers and I would stand on our front porch patiently waiting for the rusty white church bus to pull up. I'll never forget, there was one particular Sunday morning that was different from all the other Sundays of my life. I recall Ray, Lamont, and I were all anxious for the bus to arrive when it finally stopped at our house. We all got in the bus and rolled on into Saint Olive Mount Baptist Church. While on the sturdy old bus, I stared up at the tinted bluish-grey clouds with my face pressed up against the bus's frigid window, wondering, "What will this day bring?"

We arrived at Grandma Nadeya's modest little church. From the outside, all you could hear were the vibrations of musical instruments, the choir singing, and the sound of hard thumping. The thumping of feet and the clapping of hands were expressions of praise to the Lord. It was coordinated noise to acknowledge that the Holy Spirit was in the building. The music was always amazing! I felt the rhythm of the drumbeat deep down in my soul. Each Sunday, we always had to sit at the front of the church, in the third row, right next to Grandma Nadeya. If it weren't for her sending that church bus to pick us up on Sunday mornings, we would not have known anything about God.

Chapter 2: Splashing in Holy Water

Grandma Nadeya made us attend Sunday school, which I didn't like because it was too long and too boring. We had to learn the importance of the Bible characters, but all I wanted to do was clap my hands and hear the music. My favorite thing about church was when the ushers and deacons would march around the church to a song about being soldiers in God's army. The words of the song go something like:

"We are soldiers in God's army!
We have to fight, although we have to cry!
We've got to hold up the blood-stained banner!
We've got to hold it up until we die!"

After the ushers and deacons sang the words of the victorious song the first time, during the second time around, the church members would join in on the singing. Everyone singing added depth, power, and conviction to the praises being exalted throughout the building.

"We are soldiers in God's army!
We have to fight, although we have to cry!
We've got to hold up the blood-stained banner!
We've got to hold it up until we die!"

The entire church body hummed or sang the victorious song with great intensity while sitting unified and with all their attention focused on God's soldiers. I was thoroughly entertained while listening to the triumphant anthem. I greatly admired the cadence of the soldiers as they marched around the fragile yet stable tabernacle of God. I respected God's soldiers because they were international missionaries who had traveled to places like Haiti and Africa to spread the word of God. Deep in my heart, I wanted to enlist in God's army and become one of God's soldiers too.

    After the church service was over, Grandma Nadeya talked to my brothers, Ray and Lamont, about receiving salvation and getting baptized. With a sincere voice, she questioned and confirmed if they were sure that they believed "Jesus Christ rose from the dead and died on the cross for their sins." With excitement in my eyes, I watched both of my brothers nod their heads and agree that they believed in Jesus and that they were going to get saved. I begged Grandma Nadeya, "Grandma, can I get saved too?" She firmly shook her head and said, "No, Sydney Marie, you're too young,

Chapter 2: Splashing in Holy Water

you're only five years old. You have to wait until you get a little bit older. You're just a baby. You don't understand yet." I pleaded with Grandma Nadeya because I was desperate to receive love and salvation from God. I understood that being baptized meant that I would have a new life, and God would instantly wash away my sins. I was motivated to do everything that my brothers did, so I began to probe again, "Why can Ray and Lamont get saved but not me, they are only two years older than me?" Grandma Nadeya said she would think about it and that we could talk about me getting saved next week. I was determined to get saved, so I prayed to God that Grandma Nadeya would allow me to do so.

    On that same day, I repeated some words about Jesus, and I promised Grandma Nadeya that I would love Jesus. When I said those words, I meant exactly what I was saying. I really wanted to love Jesus, do the right thing, and obey my parents. I memorized the Ten Commandments and boldly said them out loud:

One, "God spoke these words saying: I am the Lord thy God, who brought you out of the land of Egypt, out of the house of bondage. Thou shalt have no other gods before Me".

Two, "Thou shalt not make unto thee any graven image or any likeness of anything that is in heaven above, or that is in the earth beneath, or that is in the water under the earth: Thou shalt not bow down thyself to them, nor serve them."

Three, "Thou shalt not take the name of the Lord thy God in vain."

Four, "Remember the sabbath day, to keep it holy. Six days shalt thou labor and do all thy work: But the seventh day is the sabbath of the Lord thy God."

Five, "Honor thy father and thy mother: that thy days may be long upon the land which the Lord thy God giveth thee."

Six, "Thou shalt not kill."

Seven, "Thou shalt not commit adultery."

Chapter 2: Splashing in Holy Water

Eight, *"Thou shalt not steal."*

Nine, *"Thou shalt not bear false witness against thy neighbor."*

Ten, *"Thou shalt not covet . . . anything that is thy neighbor's".*

Miraculously, after reciting the *Ten Commandments*, God and Grandma Nadeya answered my prayers, then somehow, I was given unique clothing necessary for all the baptism candidates. I quickly suited up in a long robe-like white gown, white socks, and white underwear. As I stood there preparing to become baptized, I was shocked that I actually convinced Grandma Nadeya that I was ready to be saved and ready to get dunked in the holy water.

The baptism experience was gratifying. It was exactly what I expected. My initiation into God's army was a true badge of honor. I had to walk into a small dark space called "the upper room," which led to the tub of holy water. As I stood in line with all the other baptism candidates, I couldn't wait until it was my turn.

Ray and Lamont were baptized before me. Then it was finally my turn. All I can remember is being submerged in the warm holy water, and water rapidly going into my nose and burning my eyes. I couldn't breathe, and my hair got all messed up. The deacon who performed the baptism left my head under the water for too long. I thought that he was trying to drown me. I was relieved when he let me up for air. I thought I was dying and on my way to heaven. Unfortunately, my parents didn't show up for the baptism, but I was super excited to tell them about the experience. I couldn't wait to get home to tell my mother the best news ever.

  After the church service was over, Grandma Nadeya took us out to lunch then dropped us off at home. As I walked through the front door, all I could see was my mother curled up lying at the bottom of the stairs. Her face was bloody and severely bruised. I cried and screamed in frustration because I knew who had attacked her. My father was nowhere in sight. It was the norm for my parents to argue and fight, so I wasn't surprised about what I saw; I was just mad as hell. The holy water had cleansed my soul, but within hours the

Chapter 2: Splashing in Holy Water

happiest moment of my life was abruptly snatched from under my feet.

I witnessed my father brutally beat my mother all the time. Sometimes I tried to stop the fights, but it just seemed like I made the conflicts worse. I wanted to protect my mother, but I couldn't because my father was too strong, and I was just too scrawny and too weak to make him stop hitting her.

While staring at my mother, as she laid on the floor abused, a massive sense of guilt burdened my soul. I knew that it was my fault that she was laying there suffering. It was all my fault because I told my father about what happened at the skating rink the night before. I opened my big mouth and told my father that a strange man was roller-skating with mom. I shared everything with my father, and I didn't know that Mom skating with some man was supposed to be a secret kept away from my father. When I innocently told him what I saw, my father was furious, but I didn't expect that he would try to kill her. Despite all the fights and beatings, I loved my father with all my heart. I was his princess, and he was my hero.

From that day on, the same day I was baptized and said yes to God, it seemed as though my mother hated me. She never really looked straight at me anymore. She despised me, and she stopped expressing her affection towards me. After that tragic event, I can't recall her saying the words "I love you" to me. She always told my younger sister, Andi, those wonderful words, and she always smiled at Andi. It was apparent to the world that Andi was the joy of my mother's life. But me, Sydney-Ann Marie, on the other hand, I was nothing. It just seemed as if I was something that a mother couldn't love. I was indeed a regret, a mistake, a misfit.

At age five, Sydney and I had mutually separated; body and spirit were detached during the baptism. I dissolved our relationship. I still loved Sydney, but all I could do is pray for her and ask God to send his angels of protection to keep her safe from any harm. On the day of my baptism, God cleansed my soul. He washed away my sins, but Sydney continued to battle with the demons that never win; they just take new shape and new form but try the same old schemes hoping to

Chapter 2: Splashing in Holy Water

break or disrupt God's sacred bond with Sydney. I am always with Sydney, but she is not always with me; we just share the same body. I am Sydney's subconscious mind, her inner self. At times, I distance myself away from her; I just observe, pray, and try to learn from her mistakes. She often forgets about the bond we have with our Heavenly Father and chooses the hard roads for us. However, because of my relentless prayers and the sovereignty of God, there is still hope for the hopeless one, and there is healing for the afflicted.

SYDNEY'S BLEU

Chapter 3: Sydney's Baggage

ʂ 3 ʂ

Chapter 3: Sydney's Baggage

Back in the early 1980s, my mother was a stay at home mom that suffered from daily domestic abuse at the hands of my father. My father, who was addicted to drugs and alcohol, hurt our entire family in one way or another. Neither of my parents went to college. They were young, raising a family with each having only a high school education.

As a young child, I remember witnessing so much negativity in my home life. "Stop Daddy, STOP hurting Mommy!" I would yell as I watched my father physically, verbally, and sexually abuse my mother. I felt helpless as, on one occasion, I watched my mother's head hit the wall so hard that it broke the drywall. I felt worthless because I was too small to help my mother escape the torture; we all were too small. All I could do was scream and cry during the abusive episodes.

I was a petite little girl, only fifty-five pounds. I wasn't strong enough to pull my father off my mother to stop the fights. Unfortunately, I couldn't stop my dad from the cyclical routine of abusing my mother.

The pain from witnessing those violent acts remained unsettled within the back of my subconscious mind. I would frequently withdraw and internally analyze the agony of defeat. I don't speak much about the events from my past because, in my mind, I failed my mother. I was a small weak little girl that couldn't do anything to protect my mother or myself. "Small, weak, stupid little girl," are the words of the record that perpetually played in my mind. To this day, I keep my distance away from my mother because of the shame that I've endured. I blocked the growth of our relationship. I've remained embarrassed that I couldn't save my mother from the abuse. The psychological trauma caused by my father's abusive behavior continues to exist.

Chapter 3: Sydney's Baggage

Along with the abusive episodes, I also watched my father smoke cocaine regularly. It was nothing to see drugs and crack pipes in my home. Each time my father engaged in smoking cocaine, he would spend every penny he had to extend the duration of being high on drugs. It was a vicious cycle that included taking everything from our home and trying to sell it all at the local pawnshop. The only thing that my dad didn't sell were my clothes. Not because he didn't try, but because the pawnshop wouldn't take it. He tried to take some of my trendier clothes and expensive shoes to the pawnshops, but the pawnshop owners wouldn't give my dad money for apparel. No pawnshop would give my dad money for things that had no actual resale value. But imagine being a child and coming home from school to see an empty house with all your clothes scattered over the front porch and lying in the front yard.

When my father's cocaine addiction escalated to the point of no return, I watched my mother gain the courage to leave my father. Although my mother struggled as a single parent to provide for four children, I watched her go to college and get an education so that she could support her family. My family went from having everything that a drug dealer could buy to having absolutely nothing. Nothing, meaning my family was on welfare; we received government assistance and survived off food stamps, powdered milk, and eating the extra thick block of welfare cheese. My family and I were indeed in poverty.

    Growing up, I scrutinized everything my parents did. I spent most of my life trying to figure out the kind of person I wanted to become. I didn't really have a particular direction in mind, but I started to listen to the feedback of those around me. My mother never advised me to go to college. She never encouraged me to get an education. What my mother did see was that I had a talent for styling hair. "Sydney, you should go to beauty school," my mom would say when she would see me fix my friend's hair or style my own effortlessly. So, I attended Robert's Beauty School from 1993 to 1995, during my junior and senior years of high school. I signed up for beauty school because I wanted to make my mother proud of me. Secretly, I deeply desired to do other things with my life. I was good at things that my

Chapter 3: Sydney's Baggage

mother didn't notice. How could I expect for her to see me, her third child? She had too many problems of her own to deal with. How could she have noticed that I was good at drawing, writing, and expressing my feelings on paper, with all her own daily turmoil?

1995 was an exciting transition year for me. I finally graduated from high school. That day could not come fast enough. I honestly didn't know if it was even going to happen because high school was a daily struggle. When my counselor told me that I had enough credits to graduate, I literally cried tears of joy. My rally at the end to do make-up work and turn in late assignments paid off. I also completed cosmetology school within the same year. I must admit, I was pretty proud of myself and eager to start my life post school.

At the age of seventeen, I began my career as a cosmetologist at my first salon job in Fremont, California. I was a shampoo assistant in a salon managed by my friend, Latoya. Latoya's sister Tracey was the true salon owner, and she desperately needed help with her customers back then. I would work at the salon every weekend to gain knowledge and earn cash gratuities from Tracey's abundant clientele.

    Within a year, I became a commissioned stylist at a salon in Oakland owned by our mother's friend, Crystal. Working in Crystal's salon didn't last long because within a few months, I followed in my mother's footsteps and relocated to Atlanta.

    I was able to transfer my hairstyling license from California to Georgia. The process was tedious because I had to retake the cosmetology exam. There was no reciprocity between the two states. After passing the Georgia cosmetology exam, I worked as an independent contractor/booth renter at a cute little salon owned by a Jamaican woman named Michelle. For several years early in my career, I had an idea of someday becoming a salon owner. I also had a wild and crazy dream of moving to New York City to become a celebrity hairstylist.

    I wanted to chase after big money. I wanted to become rich, and I wanted to earn money at a rapid pace. So, one day on a whim, I quit my job and moved to New York City to pursue my lavish dreams. Foolishly, I failed

Chapter 3: Sydney's Baggage

to give my boss, Michelle, a two-week notice, and I abandoned my established clientele, but I was headed to NYC!

I had always believed in myself; therefore, I honestly thought that I would acquire fortune and success in a big city like New York. The Big Apple is known for housing all the celebrities and up-and-coming stars. I didn't want to struggle like I did while growing up, and I didn't want to rely on a man for any support. I was afraid of being abused. The last thing I ever wanted was to endure the pain that my mother suffered. I had made a conscious decision to work for myself and create my own independence.

The day I landed in New York, I was bombarded with opportunities to party, invited to exclusive VIP events, and was able to connect with some of the hottest A-list celebrities in town. I did my thing and partied with the celebrities in hopes of landing a gig as someone's personal hairstylist. In the process, I lost myself and strayed from my true values chasing after money. I even managed to work on a few so-called high-profile clients, but there was a significant price that I had to pay, which was not worth a minute of my time.

After achieving little success and suffering from severe depression, trying to establish my career as a celebrity hairstylist, I finally left New York. In August 2011, one month before the attack of the "Twin Towers," I moved back to Georgia. In my heart, I knew that God had saved me from that tragedy because before leaving New York, my job was located only two minutes away from Times Square.

Upon returning to Atlanta, I made plans to achieve a new goal. My vision was to become a salon owner. It only took me a few months to develop a cohesive business plan, which I showed to a few people I knew, and I was able to secure a small loan. Unfortunately, the loan was given to me by a businessman who was an undercover drug dealer. The businessman that lived a double life loaned me ten thousand dollars in cash in exchange for one night of intimacy. He held up his part of the deal. But, when I made excuses and procrastinated on giving him what he was hoping for, he turned into a verbally abusive, demanding idiot. He accused me of stealing his money. He threatened to sue me in court, and he threatened to take the business from me completely.

It was quite humiliating to know what I had considered doing and almost signed up for, to try and gain success. The salon did well in the beginning. However, my success was short-lived, probably because I went about getting the capital the wrong way. Through my own mistakes, I learned that the things done for money should be carefully considered to obtain real wealth and real success. Although the proposition didn't work out as planned, I did manage to make monthly payments to pay the loan off.

My beauty salon survived for nearly five years. Unfortunately, I had to close the business because the tenant in the space connected to my unit purchased the entire building from the landlord.

The new landlord was a young red-haired Caucasian man that opened a violin shop next to my salon. He put me out of business because he needed the space to expand his violin company. Unfortunately, I had to surrender my salon space and move out. I was devastated; I felt terrible, and I felt like a failure again.

    Did I mention that I was married with children? Somewhere between moving from New York back to Atlanta, I was swept off my feet and got married. Vinny was my trusted friend, and I thought we would experience everything together. But when the salon closed and money got tight, my marriage began to decline. My husband had moved out of state, and I was left alone to raise a seven-year-old child and two newborn babies.

    Everything was falling apart, and what's most devastating is that I didn't have my business anymore. I had lost my love and my passion. The business was my lifeline; it connected me to the world. The business gave me an identity and a sense of purpose. I had no friends, but my clients had become my most trusted confidants, so when I had to close the salon, I felt as if I had lost everything that I had worked so hard for. "Here we go again, round two in the battle with depression," I remember saying out loud.

Chapter 3: Sydney's Baggage

When my husband and I couldn't afford to pay our mortgage, the light bills or water bills, that's when I filed for a divorce. I was so upset with myself because I didn't want to struggle with raising my children and not having the necessities of life. During that time, I had never heard of *postpartum depression,* but after undergoing some medical evaluations, my doctor explained to me, "Your hormones didn't have a chance to stabilize being that you had two small children ten months apart."

For about six years, after the divorce and struggling as a single parent, I suffered from double depression. I was depressed about the traumatic events from my childhood. I was depressed about the decision to divorce my husband. I was confused about my choice of having my children so close together. I questioned myself, "Why would anyone be so stupid to have children exactly ten months apart then file for a divorce?" Imagine having two babies in diapers and two babies crying at the same time; I was a pure mental train-wreck waiting to explode.

During the six years of what doctors considered as *major depression*, I did find some time to reinvent myself. I refused to pop happy pills each day of my life, but I did regularly speak to a psychologist. I scheduled regular therapy visits to talk with Dr. Shaw. Dr. Shaw was a godsend that helped me get down to the root cause of my issues. Through the therapy sessions, I was able to identify the crucial moments and individual people that neglected me as a child. Dr. Shaw helped me to create effective coping techniques, and she also advised me to change my diet and reestablish my relationship with God. With support from my family, I was able to overcome the once debilitating mental health disorder.

While battling depression, I took business management courses at Gwinnett Technical Community College. I also went back to school to get my cosmetology instructor's license. A year later, I studied massage therapy at Georgia Massage & Esthetics School, and I was able to obtain a license to practice massage therapy.

Chapter 3: Sydney's Baggage

    I had several significant opportunities to work for the best cosmetology schools and luxury hotels, but I ruined those opportunities. My attitude was horrible, and I didn't appreciate what I had. I always wanted more, but I was suffering from major depression and burnout.

    I was mad at the world and probably just angry at myself because I wasn't truly where I wanted to be in life. Back in the day, the only two dreams or goals that I ever had was to become a salon owner or a celebrity hairstylist. With full effort, I tried both of my dreams, but the end results made me feel like a failure each time I tried. Throughout the duration of my cosmetology career, I probably had over one thousand clients. At some point, I walked away from it all. I quit my job in a spa at a luxury hotel. I didn't know what was going on within myself. I stopped eating. I stopped answering my cellphone. I sent my children to go live with their father. I went into total isolation from the rest of the world. What was happening to me was unexplainable. I talked to a shrink and the pastor of my church, but nothing seemed to help. I would sleep for days at a time, and I often cried myself into pure misery.

One day after crying out to God, my life changed right before my eyes. "Sydney, I LOVE YOU exactly the way you are! Have faith and believe in MY ability to work miracles," said the audible voice. It was a word from God. On that day, I began to write my goals on paper, and I began to imagine myself doing something that I truly enjoyed. I imagined myself helping people. I had no money in the bank, no job, no friends, barely any food to eat, and no sense of direction. Then God stepped in and revealed to me His plan. All this time, I had been making so many of my own plans and getting nowhere fast. The day I surrendered my plans to the Lord and decided to put him first was the day God decided to wipe away my pain and bless my life with peace, joy, and happiness.

I'm here today to share my testimony and to encourage you to stay on the course with eyes on God. Here are a few stories from my past; Sydney's stories, full of self-discovery, and tips that I've learned throughout this journey called life.

ꙮ 4 ꙮ

Chapter 4: Me Too

Sydney met Dee on the last day of the BSU (Black Student Union) convention in San Diego. The high school she attended planned the BSU trip for the African American students to meet with (HBCUs) historically black colleges and their recruiters. Sydney was there for the wrong reasons. She had no real interest in attending college; that subject was never a topic of discussion because her mother couldn't afford it. Sydney just went on the trip to have fun and to see cute boys.

Dee was, by far, one of the most handsome boys at the convention. He was tall, dark brown-skinned, and he had wavy sun-kissed golden-brown hair. As he and Sydney walked past each other, their eyes met, and at the same time, they both said, "What's up." After a few minutes of conversation, Dee expressed that he was from

Oakland and that he would be willing to drive anywhere to spend time with Sydney. He and Sydney exchanged telephone numbers, and it was on! Sydney couldn't wait to get back home to see Dee again.

A week after meeting Dee, he and Sydney made plans to hook up. The following Friday morning, after the BSU convention, Sydney got up, got dressed, and prepared herself to go to school. Instead of catching the regular school bus, Sydney rode the city transit to the BART train station. She had skipped school once before, so she thought that this time would be no different. Dee talked her into catching the train to Oakland to see him.

Sydney boldly took the train from Fremont to East Oakland which was a 30-minute ride. She never once thought about the consequences; each day of Sydney's life, her mother worked a full-time job and a part-time job, so she would never notice that Sydney had missed a day of school. Sydney also thought that she would arrive back home at a decent time.

When Sydney reached the train stop in East Oakland, she walked out of the train station and noticed Dee leaning against the hood of a teal-green old school

Chapter 4: Me Too

nineteen sixty-six Mustang. At that moment, their eyes met again, the same way they did in San Diego, and it was on. Dee drove Sydney through the lonely streets of East Oakland then to his house. When he and Sydney arrived at his shabby little home, Dee mischievously introduced Sydney to his mother. Dee's mother was a thin little Hispanic lady with very few words to say, and a crooked grin etched on her face. Sydney was shocked by the appearance of Dee's mother. She didn't know that Dee was bi-racial; his skin tone was dark brown, similar to Sydney's complexion.

    After meeting Dee's mother, Dee and Sydney went straight into his cramped bedroom. Dee had quickly pulled out a joint that he had hidden in his top dresser drawer. He reached into his pocket, grabbed his royal-blue cigarette lighter, lit the joint, and took a massive puff of the weed. Dee offered Sydney some grass, but she refused and told him, "No, I'm not doing that." He smoked the weed some more then offered it to Sydney again. She boldly told him "no" again. This time he got close to Sydney's face, opened her mouth with his fingers, put his lips onto Sydney's lips then blew smoke directly into Sydney's mouth. Within seconds she started feeling weird, and her body became numb and lifeless. Sydney had no intention of being intimate with Dee. She just wanted to hang out and get to know him, but Dee had become overly aggressive, and his hands were all over Sydney's body. He pulled down Sydney's pants and began to touch her inappropriately; she couldn't stop the fifteen seconds of penetration.

Sydney had no control over what was happening to her. Her mind was on a different planet because the weed that Dee had blown into her mouth had been laced with PCP. Sydney didn't give Dee consent to blow smoke, laced with angel dust, in her face, yet he did it because he knew that she would get high and become vulnerable. After Dee had his way with Sydney, they got dressed then drove to Dee's friend's house. By this time, it was eight o'clock in the evening, and Sydney had totally lost track of time.

Sydney's Motorola beeper went off over a hundred times. It was Sydney's mother paging her to find out why she hadn't made it home from school yet. Sydney was hallucinating; she saw odd shapes and hues

Chapter 4: Me Too

of blue and green race across the walls. She didn't know where she was, and Dee had left her at his friend's house. Sydney managed to find a cordless phone so she could call her mother. Her mother's voice sounded subdued, yet Sydney felt the tension and anger through the phone. "Where the hell are you?" she asked. "Mom, I don't know where I'm at," Sydney replied. "What do you mean, you don't know?" Sydney's mother questioned. "Mom, I was with a boy, and he was smoking weed, and I really don't know where I'm at, and the boy I was with left me," Sydney tried to explain to her mother. "Go outside and tell me the name of the street you are on, so I can come and get you," she said. Sydney was more afraid of her mother than being left alone in someone's house that she did not know. Sydney listened to her mother and walked outside, but she was too high to find the street sign, so Sydney made up a street name. She didn't tell her mother the truth about where she was. "Mom, I'll find my way home. You don't have to come to get me." She disregarded her mother and hurried to end the phone call. Sydney walked back into the house, sat on the couch, and continued to stare at the shapes and colors moving across the walls.

When Sydney woke up, she called Dee to come to pick her up and take her home. When Dee came back to the house, he was in a different car, a stunning bright yellow convertible Cutlass Supreme Classic.

Sydney didn't mention anything about what happened at Dee's mother's house, nor did she say a word about him leaving her at his friend's house. Dee drove Sydney all the way to Fremont and dropped her off one block away from home. They said goodbye, and that was the last time Sydney saw Dee's despicable face.

As Sydney approached the front porch of where she lived, her mother was standing at the door with a black leather belt in hand. When Sydney walked into her home, Sydney had received one of the worst beatings of her entire life. Without taking a break, her mother whipped her continuously for what seemed like hours.

Sydney accepted her punishment and took ownership of her choice of skipping school, but the consequence of being date-raped was collateral damage. Sydney was ashamed and embarrassed. No woman or

Chapter 4: Me Too

girl deserves any experience like what Sydney had endured. She had been drugged and raped yet kept the incident a secret for years because she felt like it was her fault. As a teenager, Sydney kept quiet and endured the guilt of non-consensual sex. As adults, Sydney and every woman should know that nonconsensual sex is illegal and considered a violation of a woman's body. It's rape.

There are two lessons learned from this scenario: First, Sydney's irresponsible choices allowed her to get stuck in an uncomfortable situation, which yielded a negative outcome. Second, Sydney could have walked away instead of staying in the presence of someone that was choosing to do drugs. She didn't have to stay there. The moment Dee pulled his weed out, Sydney could've excused herself and asked Dee to take her back to the train station. Sydney's choice of keeping the incident a secret and not exposing Dee's offense was a disservice to society. Who knows how many other girls Dee violated using the same scheme he used to strategically take Sydney's virginity?

SYDNEY'S BLEU

ꒉ 5 ꒉ

Chapter 5: Teenage Drama

During the hot summer of 1994, Sydney met Jamal Jones when she was a junior at Irvington High School. When they met, Jamal was one of the hottest teenage rappers in California. Jamal was from Vallejo, born and raised on the southside of town. *Mac Jay* was the name the world knew him by. He was a young want-to-be street hustler with so much game that he had learned from hanging around older gangsters from his neighborhood. Of course, *Mac Jay* was a typical player and heartthrob. Most of the teenage girls from California were in-love with *Mac Jay,* or at least they all dreamed of being his girlfriend. The first time Sydney noticed *Mac Jay,* he was on TV hosting one of the popular hip-hop music shows. When *Mac Jay* spoke, his lyrics were smooth, and his style was really suave and cool. Sydney knew that one day they would meet.

Every year during the summertime, in California, Sydney and some of her friends from high school would attend *Summer Jam*, an outdoor concert where all the hottest rappers and singers would perform. *Mac Jay* was on the lineup of performers guaranteed to be at the show. When Sydney heard *Mac Jay's* name on the roster of rappers performing, she immediately telephoned her friends to confirm that they would be attending the concert. Of the four girls that Sydney had called, only two of her friends, Kesha and Kanesha, enthusiastically agreed that they would be going. After hearing their confirmation, Sydney quickly called Ticketmaster to purchase her twenty-four-dollar concert ticket for the Summer Jam.

On the day of the concert, the stars must have been aligned; just by chance, as Sydney was walking to the restroom, *Mac Jay* stopped Sydney in her tracks. "Damn, you're fine! What's your name?" *Mac Jay* asked Sydney. Sydney was the luckiest girl in the world that day. Elated by meeting the rap star, she replied, "My

Chapter 5: Teenage Drama

name is Sydney, but you can call me Syd. What's your name?" Sydney knew exactly who *Mac Jay* was. "I'm Jamal Jones. Here's my number, baby. Call me when you leave the concert," *Mac Jay* spoke confidently. Then, he handed Sydney a small piece of ripped tissue paper that had his signature and seven digits scribbled across it. Knowing that Sydney, a starstruck teenage girl, would call him, Jamal stared into Sydney's eyes then romantically kissed her on the lips. Shocked by receiving the unexpected wet kiss, Sydney blushed, took Jamal's phone number and held it close to her heart. Sydney thought to herself, "This day is unbelievable. I actually met *Mac Jay,* and he was interested in me!" That encounter with *Mac Jay* elevated Sydney's confidence level from a five up to a ten.

Mac Jay was the talk of the town; everyone in California loved his music, yet he was trying his hardest to get to know Sydney a little better. Jamal and Sydney talked on the telephone almost every day. They both expressed their desires to spend time together, but Jamal had to travel often because he had several performances, and Sydney had to attend high school, so for months, their relationship remained strictly verbal. Then on one random day, after about five months into their courtship, Jamal invited Sydney to see him perform at an underground club in San Francisco. Somehow, Sydney made her way to the club to see Jamal's performance that night. When Sydney arrived at the club, the first thing she did was head to the restroom so that she could change her clothes. Sydney left out of her house in regular workout clothes because if she had gone out of the house in her sexy outfit, her mom would have known that she was up to something. While in the restroom, Sydney quickly went into a bathroom stall to change out of her gym clothes. Sydney eased into a short black leather miniskirt and put on a shiny gold beaded tank top; then, she slipped into her glossy black patent leather two-inch heeled pumps. Sydney dusted her oily face with a bronze press powder and enhanced her dry lips with a plum shade of rouge lipstick. Sydney finished primping in the mirror, stuffed her gym clothes into her backpack, exited the restroom. She then began to strut through the crowd towards the stage. As Sydney got closer to the stage, Jamal greeted her with his sexy

Chapter 5: Teenage Drama

gangster smile. Over the booming music, Jamal shouted, "Stay right here. I'm performing next. You're leaving with me when this is over?" "Yeah, I'm going with you," Sydney replied.

Jamal Jones got on that stage and mystically turned into *Mac Jay*. Sydney loved *Mac Jay*; she loved his music. She loved his style. Sydney loved both personas; Jamal, the rapper, and the teenage gangster. While he lyrically dominated the stage, Sydney blushed innocently. She was feeling the vibe. So, she bobbed her head and snapped her fingers to the rhythm of the bass drum. Jamal rapped and sang about five different tracks from his first album, and the crowd went crazy, including Sydney. The show was the bomb! The entire time Jamal was on stage, his eyes stayed fixated on Sydney as if he were rapping his lyrics directly to her. Sydney was on cloud nine, cheerful like an immature child on Christmas morning.

Sydney and Jamal left the club together after his performance was over. Jamal was hungry, so they drove through the Bay Area and stopped at *Fat Boy's* restaurant to get a bite to eat. Jamal ordered chilly-cheese fries and a cherry slush. Sydney only ordered a small bottle of water because she was too embarrassed to eat food in front of Jamal. Sydney didn't want Jamal to notice how big the gap in between her teeth was, so she knew not to eat in front of someone like him. Sydney was really hungry, but she was ok. As Jamal shoved chilly-cheese fries down his face, Sydney slowly sipped the bottled water to suppress some of her hunger pains. As Sydney ignored the sounds of her growling stomach, all she could think of was Jamal. He was the coolest dude ever; he was a famous teenage rap star, and he was Sydney's boyfriend.

After Jamal guzzled down the sloppy fries and slurped the last drop of his cherry slush, he and Sydney exited *Fat Boy's* restaurant. Jamal cuffed Sydney as he walked with his arm over Sydney's boney shoulder, physically expressing that she had belonged to him. Sydney and Jamal instantaneously became lovers. "This cannot be true. My boyfriend is a famous rapper!" Sydney shallowly said underneath her breath. Sydney was living out her fantasy.

Chapter 5: Teenage Drama

Later that evening, Jamal rented a shabby room at some run-down low budget motel. Although the room was crappy, Jamal did everything to make Sydney feel like she was in a more beautiful hotel. Insinuating that he was low on cash, Jamal promised Sydney, "Once I switch record labels and sign my new record deal, I'll take you to nicer places." Sydney was in a trance, so she believed every lyric uttered from Jamal's lips.

During intimacy, Jamal's expired protective latex had ripped. The magnitude of his body parts and the circumference of the protective latex were not compatible; Sydney felt the exact moment it ruptured. That night they both knew that there was a possibility that Sydney had become pregnant. Jamal's bodily fluids waded inside of Sydney, and shortly after, she began to feel nauseous. Within the same hour, Sydney complained of having an upset stomach, so she and Jamal left the motel and decided that Sydney should go home. While driving Sydney home, Jamal had to pull over on the side of Interstate 880, so Sydney could vomit. When they finally arrived at Sydney's house, Jamal helped Sydney out of his car, hugged her, and told her, "Syd, you'll be ok." Sydney didn't respond; she just hugged him back then casually walked into her home.

    The next day, there was no doubt in Sydney's mind that she had been impregnated. She was convinced early on that she was experiencing all the apparent signs of pregnancy. Soon, her feet became visibly swollen, and she couldn't hold down any food. She began to lose a lot of weight and vomiting each morning before going to school had become her private ritual. Sydney's face and the back of her neck strangely developed small acne-like bumps. She craved weird food combinations such as peanut butter and French fries, and she wanted ranch dressing on everything.

    The following month, Sydney's menstrual cycle didn't arrive. Missing a monthly period was not a conclusive confirmation of pregnancy, so Sydney secretly purchased an over-the-counter home pregnancy kit. In the privacy of her home, Sydney carefully followed each step included in the instructions of the pregnancy test. She urinated on the absorbency stick, waited two minutes for the results, then called Jamal with the news. After the second ring, he answered the

Chapter 5: Teenage Drama

telephone, "Hello." "Hey," said Sydney in a low voice. "I already know what you're calling to tell me. I already know. You're pregnant," Jamal said in a frustrated tone. "Yeah," said Sydney, in the same low voice. Then Jamal angrily demanded, "You need to go have an abortion. I'm not ready to take care of no kids. I live with my mother. I like you, but I don't love you. I'm not trying to be with you like that, and I'm not about to marry you. So, what are you going to do, Syd?" "I love this baby. I'm not having an abortion!" said Sydney, with tears in her eyes and the same low voice. Without saying good-bye, Jamal abruptly hung up the phone.

    Sydney tried to hide the pregnancy from her mother for as long as she could, but her mother found out from Ms. Snow, Sydney's third-period science teacher. Ms. Snow called Sydney's mother and sent Sydney home because Sydney couldn't stop throwing up. The moment Sydney arrived at home, her mother looked at her in disbelief and said, "If you are pregnant, you cannot live here. You have to move out." Teary-eyed Sydney didn't respond to her mother's comments; she kept quiet, then went to her bedroom and closed the door. Sydney didn't have any emotional support. Neither Jamal nor her mother was there for her. Jamal stopped accepting Sydney's phone calls, and Sydney's mother basically told her that she had to move out. Sydney was extremely stressed, and she felt like she was under an immense amount of pressure. Sydney must have cried herself to sleep every night.

Sydney's first eight weeks of pregnancy were extremely difficult. Due to morning sickness and sleepless nights, Sydney couldn't manage to regularly attend school without being tardy, falling asleep in class, or vomiting during the lessons.

On a cold Saturday afternoon during week eleven of Sydney's pregnancy, she rested in bed unmotivated and fatigued as she approached the end of her first trimester. While Sydney laid comfortably, she thought of the perfect name for her unborn child. "I'll call it Jalisa if it's a girl or Jamal if it's a boy." Amid her thoughts, all of a sudden muffled rumbling sounds, abdominal cramping, and severe lower back pains began to violently rupture the contents within Sydney's womb. As red and brown bloody mucus rushed out of Sydney's

Chapter 5: Teenage Drama

vagina, she instinctually cradled her stomach. Engulfed in pain, Sydney crawled to the bathroom and sorrowfully passed chunks of her fetus's flesh down into the toilet. There was blood everywhere, so Sydney stayed seated on the toilet to stop the blood from gushing onto the floor. While sitting in the bathroom, Sydney hurried to call her cousin. "Melba, please help me. I'm in pain! I'm losing my baby! I'm losing a lot of blood! It's bloody everywhere! I don't know what to do! Please come help me!" Sydney frantically cried out to her cousin.

Melba immediately arrived at Sydney's home, shocked by the amount of blood trailing from Sydney's bedroom throughout the bathroom floor, Melba screamed, "What the hell, Oh my god! We need to hurry and get you to the hospital!" Melba reached into the closet, grabbed five old bath towels, and began handing the linen to Sydney. "Here, wrap the towels around your waist and in between your legs! They will help with the bleeding." Melba hysterically instructed Sydney on what to do. Melba was terrified by the sight of so much blood. She quickly helped Sydney out of the house, and into her navy-blue Mustang. Melba anxiously sped down the street to rush Sydney to the nearest emergency room. When they arrived at the hospital, Melba ran inside to get assistance because Sydney needed help with getting out of the car. Two of the emergency room employees quickly ran outside to help Sydney exit the blood-filled vehicle. After safely removing her, they placed Sydney in a vacant emergency room while Melba signed the paperwork to check Sydney into the hospital. Within fifteen minutes, the physicians transferred Sydney to an operating room to perform emergency surgery. Sydney endured two hours of operation and was given no anesthesia. She felt dismayed as the physicians scraped and vacuumed the remnants from the walls of her uterus. Upon completion of the D&C surgery, the medical staff gave Sydney a written prescription for antibiotics, apologized to her about the loss of the baby then nonchalantly sent Sydney on her way. Upon release, she stayed calm then broke the silence with wailing as she called Jamal to inform him of everything that happened. "I lost the baby today," Sydney explained as she tried to hold back her tears. During that phone call, Jamal

Chapter 5: Teenage Drama

comforted Sydney, "Don't worry Syd, you'll be alright. Everything between us is cool. We're ok".

The traumatic incident scorned Sydney for life. After experiencing the miscarriage, Sydney thought that she was barren and would never become a mother. Sydney lost her unborn child because of the unwarranted stress placed upon her by Jamal and her mother. Sydney placed the blame of the tragedy on both of them. Losing the baby was mostly her mother's fault as she saw it. Sydney felt a lot of resentment towards her mother. She hated that her mother neglected her during a time of need. Jamal and Sydney's mother treated her like crap during the pregnancy, yet within the depths of Sydney's heart, although very angry with him, she still loved Jamal.

As if nothing life-altering had happened, Jamal and Sydney went back to being boyfriend and girlfriend again. Sydney continued being intimate with him every weekend or every chance she could get to Vallejo.

After many late-night conversations, Jamal and Sydney decided that the distance between them was not conducive to a real relationship. He was a rapper focused

61

on establishing his music career, and Sydney was a high school student struggling to graduate. Right before graduating from high school, Sydney and Jamal had officially broken up. Still, they continued to exchange their life stories over the telephone.

Jamal frequently called Sydney to tell her all the details concerning his major record deal. "Syd, you remember a year ago when we met? Remember I told you about the record label that wanted to sign me?" "Yeah sure, I remember you were mentioning something about a label," Sydney replied. "Guess what! It finally happened! I signed a dope-ass contract! I'm moving out of my mother's house. I bought this plush two-bedroom penthouse-condo," Jamal bragged to Sydney. "What city are you moving to?" Sydney asked. "The suburbs of Berkeley," answered Jamal. "When are you going to come over?" Jamal asked Sydney. "Give me your address, I'll come over next week," Sydney told him.

A week went by, and Sydney drove to Berkley to see Jamal's new condo. Sydney entered the parking deck of the high-rise condo building to gain access to the securely guarded facility. Sydney had to provide Jamal's

Chapter 5: Teenage Drama

first and last name then show the concierge her driver's license to get access onto the elevator. When Sydney finally arrived at Jamal's penthouse, she pushed the gold-plated doorbell. After about thirty seconds of waiting, Jamal opened the oversized steel door. Sydney walked into Jamal's chicly decorated loft. "Wow! Did you have an interior designer help you decorate this place?" Sydney probed. "Yeah, the new record label paid this design firm from San Francisco to select every piece of contemporary furniture in this pad. I just told them that I wanted everything to be brand new, and all white. To add a little bit of contrast to the decor, I had to bring my albino snake from my mother's house," Jamal proudly explained while he gave Sydney a tour of his condo. Sydney followed Jamal as he walked through the living room over to the coffee table, which displayed his mice-eating reptile lying inside a glass cage. "Do you like this centerpiece?" Jamal pressed Sydney for her honest opinion. "It's a snake, no! It looks interesting, but I don't like snakes," Sydney firmly said as she backed away from the ten-foot-long serpent. After Sydney finished the tour of Jamal's penthouse, she expressed to him, "Jamal, your place looks nice. I'm proud of you! Thanks for the tour. I need to head out. I have a few errands to run before it gets late".

Jamal invited Sydney to his condo often. When she would get there, he would be high, intoxicated, and in the mood for wild pleasure. "Why do you always drink Hennessy and smoke weed?" Sydney asked. "The weed makes me calm, and the Hennessy makes me wild. I need both to stay balanced," he replied. Intimacy with Jamal lasted forever; it never ended. Jamal enjoyed chasing Sydney around his condo. He and Sydney would wrestle on the floor, and he would take pleasure in biting her flesh. Jamal was like a wild animal. He was always very aggressive; intimacy with him was more like a dog chasing its toy around until to the point of exhaustion. While being intimate, he would smack Sydney's behind so hard that she would notice red and blue visible bruising on her body.

Six months after Jamal moved into his condo, Sydney was preparing for a move of her own. Sydney called Jamal to set a date to see him and say her final farewells. "Hey Jamal, if you're in town, I'll stop by

Chapter 5: Teenage Drama

your condo in a few days to see you." "Cool," Jamal agreed.

  Two days before visiting Atlanta, Sydney went to Jamal's condo for the last time. Surprisingly they were not intimate. They just talked, laughed, and reminisced about life. Sydney enthusiastically told Jamal about her plans, "I'm leaving the Bay. I'm heading to Atlanta, and I'm probably going to move to the "ATL" with my mother in a couple of months. I'm going to visit this week to see if I like it." Jamal's response and final words to Sydney were, "Syd. I can see you dancing at the Blue Flame or Magic City when you get to Atlanta." "What is that? What's Magic City?" Sydney questioned cluelessly. "It's a strip club," Jamal replied. "No, no, I'm not. I'm going to be the owner of a beauty salon!" Sydney firmly corrected him and rolled her eyes with a disgusted look on her face. After digesting Jamal's insulting words, Sydney quickly got up and reluctantly hugged him. They said their good-byes; Jamal and Sydney never saw each other nor spoke to one another ever again. Jamal's words about Magic City were quite painful for Sydney....

Sydney's feelings were hurt to know that all Jamal thought that she would ever do with her life is become a stripper at Magic City. "How dare anyone try to speak those wretched words over my life. I'll show him," Sydney thought to herself. She used his negative words as motivation and fuel to pursue her dreams.

Chapter 6: Love and War with a Muslim

In 1995 on a hot Sunday afternoon while hanging out at Lake Merit in East Oakland, Sydney met a Muslim guy by the name of Malik. This encounter was during Sydney's senior year of high school and soon after dealing with Mac Jay. As Sydney and her friends casually walked around Lake Merit with their short shorts on, Sydney and Malik accidentally bumped into each other, and their eyes met. Malik had been strolling around the lake with his cousin Tone and his best friend, Joe. "Excuse me, Beautiful; my apologies," Malik said as he found his footing and looked at Sydney. He felt a tap on his shoulder from Tone. All three of the young men were staring at Sydney. Tone stepped to Sydney and said, "Hey, can I have your number?" Sydney looked him up and down then said, "No, you can't, I don't think that's a good idea." Sydney was not attracted to Tone, nor did she like his style. Tone's appearance was too thuggish. His demeanor was as if he was permanently up to no good. Turned off by Tone, Sydney slowly gazed over at Malik, and he was staring deep into her eyes, "Well what about me, can I have your number," Malik asked. Sydney looked him up and down and said, "Yes. You can have my number."

Malik explained to Sydney that he was practicing the Muslim religion under the direction of Minister Louis Farrakhan. He mentioned that he had recently connected to the Nation of Islam; he was one of the five-percenters. He explained that his name had been changed from Darrell to Malik when he converted his faith from Christianity to Islamic beliefs.

Malik was very tall and handsome. He had a lovely pecan-tan brown complexion, but his eyes were dark, black, and cold. What attracted Sydney to Malik was that he had enough confidence to ask for Sydney's telephone number after he watched her reject his cousin. Sydney and Malik exchanged numbers and immediately conversed on the telephone for hours. Every

Chapter 6: Love and War with a Muslim

conversation they had was in-depth. They spoke about spirituality and their different views and opinions on everything from goals to food and politics.

On their first date, Malik borrowed his cousin's green Ford pickup truck to take Sydney out. He took Sydney to the Muslim bakery, a place that gave reformed criminals stable employment. The bakery was Malik's first job, where he worked and spent a lot of his time. Malik proudly showed Sydney off to his co-workers. He was so honored to have Sydney in his company. Sydney and Malik ate at the Muslim bakery because Malik didn't have any money to take Sydney out on a real date. Malik made bean pies for a living, but Sydney didn't care because she was impressed that he had a legitimate job. Sydney was very intrigued by Malik because he was different. Malik was a member of the Nation of Islam, he read lots of books, and he had an independent mind. Malik wanted something out of life, and he wanted Sydney to be right there by his side. Before he and Sydney were ever intimate, he would pray to Allah that Sydney would become the mother of his children.

Malik invited Sydney to visit the mosque that he regularly attended, so she did. Sydney liked what she heard when she attended the Muslim meetings, so she soaked up all the knowledge. There were times when Sydney did not agree with all the views expressed during the sessions, yet she continued to attend. To try and impress Malik, Sydney would wrap her hair in scarves, wore long skirts, and read every book that Malik placed in her hands. Malik wouldn't allow Sydney to eat pork around him, but she secretly ate it whenever they weren't together. Malik hated the way Sydney looked with makeup on her face. He hated it so much that he would take his hand and wipe the makeup entirely off her face then say, "Your face is naturally beautiful. Why do you want to put that whale fat on your face? You look like a clown with that stuff on." He would build Sydney up and tear her down all at the same time.

Despite her mother's warnings and advice, Sydney continued to spend much of her time with Malik. Sydney's mother repeatedly warned her, "You're going to end up pregnant. Keep on messing around with that boy." Sydney tried to convince her, "Mom, he's

Chapter 6: Love and War with a Muslim

different. He is Muslim. We are not going to have sex. He wants to marry me and have a family with me." Sydney didn't listen to her mother's warning. One year after graduating from high school, her mother's exact words became her reality. Sydney had gotten pregnant.

Malik had prayed to Allah for a child, so Sydney believed that Malik was going to marry her, and they would have a beautiful family together. During Sydney's pregnancy, she learned about several other women that Malik was fooling around with. One night, Sydney had called Malik twenty times, and when he finally answered the phone, Sydney heard a girl's voice in the background. Enraged by the sound of a female's voice, Sydney rapidly drove over to Malik's apartment because she was determined to find out the truth. Sydney banged on the door furiously until Malik finally came out. Sydney anxiously asked him, "What's going on?" Malik responded to Sydney's question, "Go back home. I didn't answer my phone because I have a female friend over." Sydney left Malik's apartment but not without a brutal fight. Sydney tried to go into Malik's home to confront the girl that he was dealing with. Without any luck, Malik and Sydney tussled at his front door, and he restrained Sydney from going inside. From the window of Malik's bedroom, the girl in the apartment patiently watched Malik and Sydney wrestle like animals. That night was truly humiliating for Sydney. When the truth finally surfaced, Sydney learned that the girl inside of Malik's apartment was his brother's wife. Malik was having an affair with his brother's wife, and he had also gotten her pregnant. Eventually, Malik's brother and his wife divorced. It was a ridiculously messy situation. Not only did Malik get his brother's wife pregnant, he also got two other women pregnant. Malik was about to become the father of four children by four different women.

Despite the cheating scandals, Sydney was absurdly in-love with Malik. She and Malik always fantasized about marriage and having many children together, but when Sydney found out about all the other women, she knew that Malik was not the man for her. Many women were in heavy rotation in Malik's bedroom, so Sydney decided to move with her mother to

Atlanta once she realized that she couldn't have a future with Malik.

    During Sydney's pregnancy, Malik came to Atlanta to visit her. He wanted to work things out with Sydney, and he promised Sydney that he only loved her, and he promised Sydney that they would get married after she had the baby. Sydney was only nineteen years old and was pregnant with Malik's first child, so she fell for Malik's lies. Malik never stopped cheating or creeping around with various women. During his visit to Atlanta, he stayed at the apartment with Sydney and her mother. The first two days of Malik's visit, he and Sydney had a great time, but he refused to be intimate with Sydney. She didn't mind because she was so happy that Malik was there, and he was experiencing the pregnancy with her. Each time the baby would kick, or the imprint of the baby's elbow would graze across Sydney's stomach, Malik would stare in sheer amazement. On the third day of Malik's visit, Sydney was scheduled to work at A&P Supermarket, where she secured her position as a cashier. Sydney was so excited that Malik had come to Atlanta to be with her. She decided to go home during her lunch break to see her man, Malik. Right when Sydney walked into the house, Malik quickly hung up the telephone.

One second later, the phone rang. Sydney answered the phone, and it was a girl named Shaneta. Shaneta tried to explain to Sydney why she was calling for Malik, so Sydney went completely off on him. Sydney hung up the phone, then Shaneta called back. Sydney allowed Malik the opportunity to clear things up concerning this Shaneta girl. In a demanding voice, Malik convinced Shaneta to tell Sydney that nothing was going on between the two of them except for the fact that they lived together. Shaneta went on continuously telling Sydney her story. Finally, Sydney just hung up the phone. Sydney knew that Shaneta was lying to her.

Sydney tried to calm down and gave Malik some time to get his story together. Sydney urgently needed to relieve her bladder, so she got up to use the bathroom. As she walked into the bathroom, she noticed a box of *Kill Crab Lice* and a small rake-like thing. Sydney asked Malik, "Is this your stuff? What is this for?" Sydney had never seen anything like it. Malik replied, "I think I got

Chapter 6: Love and War with a Muslim

crabs from using the towels in the hotel." Sydney asked him, "Let me see. Pull down your pants." Malik came into the bathroom and pulled down his underwear. "Why did you shave off all of your pubic hair," Sydney questioned. As soon as Malik began to make up a lie, it all started to make sense. Sydney figured it out; Malik was sleeping around and got crabs. That's why he didn't want to be intimate with Sydney. "Get out," Sydney yelled at the top of her lungs. Sydney started throwing Malik's crab medicine at him and threw all Malik's things out of her mother's apartment. In the heat of the moment, Malik and Sydney began to fight, and Sydney didn't win. After the brawl was over, Sydney walked away with a black eye and two bloody busted lips. That was the last day Sydney ever spoke to Malik. On the day Sydney gave birth to their child, Sydney's mother called Malik to tell him the news. A day later, Malik arrived at the hospital with another woman to see his firstborn child.

After the birth of Sydney and Malik's child, their relationship dwindled down to nothing. Although Malik and Sydney had cut all lines of communication,

Sydney's mother secretly met up with Malik so that the child could have a relationship with his father. For years Sydney's mother continued to schedule one-hour visitation meetups. In her mind, she was doing the child and Malik a favor by trying to help them form a father-son bond.

It took Sydney about seven years to truly forgive Malik and to get over her anger for the Muslim that she once loved. Sydney wakes up each morning, and thanks God for her beautiful love child. She also thanks God for giving her the strength and courage to leave the volatile relationship that she and Malik had cultivated. God's grace and mercy would not allow Sydney to linger in any type of relationship with Malik, the Muslim that she adored.

Chapter 7: Riding Dirty

ꔷ 7 ꔷ

Chapter 7: Riding Dirty

Sydney met Carlos in the parking lot of a popular hangout spot, Club 112, in Atlanta. As Sydney exited the club, she started walking towards her car. Out of nowhere, this guy rolled up beside her in a black S500 Mercedes Benz. "Shawty, what's up? You got a man? Come here. Can I talk to you for a minute?" he yelled through the window. "You come here, get out of your car and come to me if you want to talk to me!" Sydney yelled back at him. When the guy got out of his Benz, Sydney noticed that he was her exact height and her exact skin tone. Carlos was clean-cut, had a low bald-fade, and he was fresh to the tee except for when he opened his mouth; all his teeth were outlined in gold, and he had diamonds ingrained in each tooth. Carlos looked like the typical drug pusher, and Sydney knew he had no real job but was loaded with cash.

Sydney reluctantly exchanged numbers with Carlos. Later in the week, Carlos took Sydney out to the movies. Their date went well, and he dropped Sydney off at home. Before Carlos left, he asked, "Can I come inside to use your bathroom?" Sydney said, "Sure." While inside Sydney's cute little one-bedroom apartment, Carlos went into the bathroom, closed the door, pulled out his weed, broke it up into meager pieces then rolled up a blunt.

There was an unusual odor emanating from the direction of the bathroom. Sydney suspected that something weird was happening. As she walked towards the restroom, she began to choke. Smoke and fumes quickly encroached her lungs and invaded every square foot of her tiny apartment. Carlos was blazing ganja branches in Sydney's bathroom, and she got a contact high just standing in her kitchen, waiting for him to exit the lavatory. Under the influence of hash, Sydney consented to have a relationship with Carlos. Every time

Chapter 7: Riding Dirty

they met up, hemp always found its way into the equation.

    Carlos was a big-time dope dealer. He used to drive dope from Atlanta to all the surrounding states. Somehow, Carlos found a way into Sydney's heart. Carlos was exciting, he lived on the edge, and his behavior was always unpredictable. He was full of energy and would light up whenever he was around Sydney. He knew that she was an honest and trustworthy woman. He also knew that Sydney was stupidly in love with him. On the weekends, Carlos would call Sydney early in the morning and promise Sydney that he was on his way to her house. Hours would pass by then Carlos would call again and tell Sydney that he was on his way. This would go on for days, and Sydney trusted him every time. Finally, Carlos would show up and tell Sydney some bizarre story of why it took him so long to get to her house. Sydney would get dressed, sit in the house each day, and wait on him for hours. Sometimes she would fall asleep waiting for Carlos, and then he would knock on her door in the wee hours of the night. Sydney felt like it was worth the wait because each moment with Carlos was amazing; he was always a ton of fun, and he did everything to make Sydney laugh. His anatomy was magnificent, and he was skilled at making Sydney weak-in-the-knees. She couldn't walk for at least a day after spending time with Carlos.

During one hot summer, Sydney went on a road trip with Carlos to South Carolina. They took their time and cruised on into the city of Columbia. Carlos started off driving, but once they approached the South Carolina state line, he asked Sydney to drive the remainder of the trip. When they pulled over on the side of the interstate, Carlos opened the trunk of his car to adjust a package that he had in the back. Sydney questioned, "What's in the package." Carlos answered, "It's a gift for my cousin." Sydney asked again, "What is it though?" Carlos replied, "It's nothing important. You'll see when we get to the hotel." When they finally arrived at the hotel, he handed Sydney the package and said, "Be very careful, do not drop this!" As they walked inside the hotel, Sydney was full of curiosity. Carlos quickly paid sixty-eighty dollars for the hotel room and rushed to go inside with the package that Sydney was holding. She

Chapter 7: Riding Dirty

couldn't wait to see what was in the package. Before opening the box, Carlos rolled a blunt, got high, then began to hug and kiss Sydney passionately. After their quick, intimate moment, he told Sydney to turn on the shower. She did as he asked; they both showered, washed up, and Carlos quickly got out of the steamy bathroom. Sydney stayed in the shower a few minutes longer. When she stepped out and began to dry herself off, she noticed Carlos cutting and weighing something white on a scale. Sydney instantly became paranoid as Carlos explained what he was doing. Sydney had never seen anything like that in her life. It was a huge white slab of cocaine.

Sydney didn't ask any questions. She just kneeled down and began to pray to God, "Please Lord! Don't let me get caught with him. Lord, please! If you get me out of this, I will never get in the car with Carlos ever again". Carlos said to her, "Sydney, get up, what are you doing. Just chill, everything is cool!" Sydney didn't know what to do. Her heart was racing. She began to pace back and forth in front of the hotel window. Sydney had made up in her mind that surely this was the day that she would be going to jail. Sydney thought that she was going to be a part of a huge drug bust.

As Carlos continued to cut, weigh, and bag the cocaine, Sydney's paranoia grew worst. All she could visualize was the SWAT team breaking into their hotel room, through the window, and taking her to jail. She figured that Carlos would lie and put everything off on her because she was the dummy driving the vehicle and holding the package as they walked into the hotel. Surely the hotel parking lot had surveillance cameras, and Sydney had been videotaped driving the car and holding the box of dope. "My life was over," Sydney thought.

Carlos received an alert on his beeper; it was the call that he was waiting for. He and Sydney abruptly left that hotel, they met up with some guy at a gas station, then followed the guy to a vacant house. "Freddy, my main man, what's up? What you got for me," the guy asked Carlos as they walked into the vacant house. Sydney didn't see it happen, but she knew that an illegal transaction was made. When Carlos returned to the car, he no longer had the package, and he counted multiple one-hundred-dollar bills as Sydney drove them back to

Chapter 7: Riding Dirty

Atlanta. Out the corner of her eye, Sydney watched Carlos count fifty thousand dollars. "Why did that guy call you Freddy?" Sydney asked. "Sydney, why do you ask so many damn questions? Chill out, boo," Carlos replied in a nonchalant tone. The remainder of the drive back home, Sydney stayed silent. She didn't trust Carlos anymore. Sydney really didn't know who she was dealing with, Carlos or Freddy. She knew he was a d-boy, but she really didn't know to what extent. She thought Carlos probably sold weed since he smoked it so much, but Sydney really had no clue about the cocaine. She didn't want to be anywhere near that mess.

When Carlos and Sydney arrived back in Atlanta, Sydney thanked God, and she kindly sent Carlos on his way. The minute Carlos backed out of her driveway; she deleted his telephone number from her cellphone. Sydney never wanted to see Carlos again. Carlos had put Sydney's life in jeopardy, and she didn't appreciate him not being honest with her.

Later that same night, Sydney laid on her sofa, turned on the television, and began to surf through all the channels. Sydney's comfort was immediately disturbed when she noticed a picture of Carlos's face on the local news station. The news anchor reported about a major drug bust in southwest Atlanta. Sydney watched a lady in handcuffs being escorted out of Carlos's home. In bold letters, the word "WANTED" was plastered above a picture of Carlos's face. Sydney listened to the news in awe as the reporter reiterated what happened. "At five o'clock this afternoon, Atlanta police raided the home of the alleged mastermind of the South Georgia drug cartel. Ringleader Fredrick Carlos Smith escaped the shootout, leaving two officers dead and two officers wounded. His wife Natasha Monique Smith was found in the basement of their home with two million dollars in cash, and one hundred kilos of cocaine." Before it could clearly register in Sydney's mind what was happening, Carlos was knocking at her door, saying, "Sydney, let me in! Baby, I just want to say goodbye, I'm going out of the states for a little while. I just came to see you before I leave."

Sydney was too afraid to open the door, and she was more interested in what she heard on the news. Carlos's wife, Natasha, was arrested. Sydney didn't

Chapter 7: Riding Dirty

know that Carlos was married. Sydney thought that Natasha might have been one of Carlos's girlfriends, but she really didn't believe that Carlos was married. Natasha had called Sydney's number a couple of times, talking trash, and now Sydney was watching Natasha on the news being arrested. As Carlos continued to knock on Sydney's door, she went to the living room to peek out of the window and check to see if any police cars were out there. When Sydney recognized that Carlos's Benz was the only car in sight, she decided to let him in. With a look of disappointment on her face, she stared at Carlos and waited to hear what he had to say. He confidently said, "Sydney, don't worry about nothing, I'm flying out to Jamaica tonight. Everything is ok, don't worry about nothing. I need you to hold this money for me". "No, Carlos, I'm not doing that, you need to leave! What happened at your house? The police are looking for you. You need to leave!" Sydney told him boldly. Carlos placed a black leather bag, full of money, on Sydney's kitchen table. "It's two-hundred grand. I need you to hold this for me. If the feds ask you questions, tell them you don't know anything. I know you got my back

Sydney. I trust you." Carlos kissed Sydney on her forehead then walked out.

    The police never found Carlos. He got away. Natasha took the case for him. She was sentenced to prison for fifteen years. The feds never tried to contact Sydney. The police didn't come to her house. Sydney was physically free, but her mind was in bondage. Sydney's mental state was horrible. Every day all she thought about was the police coming to arrest her. She was more paranoid than she had ever been before. Carlos ruined her life.

    Sydney couldn't eat, sleep, or trust anyone. She needed to talk to someone, but she had no one to count on. She couldn't tell anyone what was going on. Sydney was too afraid that if she confided in anyone that they would turn her in or try to steal Carlos's money from her. Her mind was almost gone. Sydney thought that the feds were watching her. She knew that her phone was tapped. She just didn't understand why the police had not questioned her. "Maybe the police are just waiting to arrest me," Sydney thought regularly. "Maybe the feds were still gathering enough evidence to connect me to

Chapter 7: Riding Dirty

Carlos and prosecute me," she pondered. Each day Sydney lived in fear; she was terrified of going to jail.

To protect herself, Sydney moved out of her one-bedroom apartment. She didn't want Carlos or the feds to know where she lived, so she rented a cute little house in a quiet neighborhood in the suburbs of northern Georgia. A month after Sydney moved, she found out that she was pregnant. Carlos was the only man that she had been dealing with, so Sydney knew that she was pregnant by him. Six months into her pregnancy, Sydney received a collect phone call from Carlos. She hesitated before accepting the call; then, the operator connected them. Sydney held the phone quietly, paranoid that the call was being recorded, then calmly sighed.

"Sydney, are you there?" Carlos asked. "Yeah," Sydney replied with hesitation in her voice. "Don't say nothing, just listen! I had to turn myself in. I got a good lawyer, so I know I'll be out soon. My lawyer said I'll probably only have to serve a few years. I'll be out in no time though. How are you, Sydney?" He asked. Sydney responded, "Carlos, I'm six months pregnant with your baby." "Stop playing, Sydney," he replied. "I'm not playing," Sydney said. "You can't have that baby. I don't know when I'm getting out of here. You need to get an abortion before it's too late." Carlos demanded. "Sydney, I've been selling dope since I was fourteen years old. This is my life. I don't know anything else. You don't want to have that baby. I won't be around. I already have five kids that don't have their daddy. You're a smart girl. I know you'll make the right decision." In disbelief of what she was hearing, Sydney quickly hung up the phone in his face.

 The next day Carlos called Sydney back and asked if she would come to visit him in jail. He said that he needed to talk to her, in person, about some business. Sydney knew precisely what he wanted to talk about; he was calling about the money. Sydney didn't go to the jailhouse to see Carlos. Instead, she went to have an abortion. Sydney used some of the money that she held for Carlos to pay for the termination procedure. With the rest of the funds, Sydney opened an upscale salon in the suburbs, north of Atlanta. Sydney knew that Carlos would be in prison for years, so she did what she had to do. Sydney got her business going, rented some salon

Chapter 7: Riding Dirty

booths to other hairstylists, and made a way for herself to survive.

SYDNEY'S BLEU

♌ 8 ♌

Chapter 8: Dreams of Death

Over fifty thousand people showed up at Sydney's funeral. This diverse group included relatives from her mother and father's family, hundreds of cops, detectives, and the sheriff from the Atlanta police department. All the hairstylists that worked for her or worked with her were there. Most of her lovers and ex-boyfriends, her children's father, her ex-husbands, lots of dope dealers and killers, and thousands of Sydney's clients were in attendance. This varied group showed up to pay their last respects. Some people came to the funeral because there had never in life been a homicide so cruelly committed. And then, there were some people who came to Sydney's funeral just to see who would show up.

This was Sydney's first dream ever where she was watching herself laying in a coffin dead. Usually, in her dreams, Sydney would escape death, and normally the bad guys would never shoot her or kill her. Sydney listened as people talked about her and viewed her lifeless body. Some gossiped about her past, and they all speculated about who could have committed such a horrible crime. Sydney's mother cried openly, but she kept her head down during the entire service.

As Sydney watched her own funeral, Sydney's sentiments were, "I always knew that I would die a tragic death, but I never thought that my life would end like this. For years I've had the same recurring dream that I was always in the wrong place at the wrong time, and I was always ducking bullets. Now I know why Grandma Nadeya cried so much and prayed so often. She feared that someday this would happen." God must have shown Grandma Nadeya signs that Sydney's life would end this way. She warned Sydney and cautioned her that if Sydney didn't live her life the right way, Sydney's reward would be an eternal hell. Sydney said to herself, "If I could turn back the time, I would have lived the way that Grandma Nadeya tried to instill in me. I had my chance. Now it's too late." Sydney pleaded with God. She gave a detailed account of her recurring dreams as if she were trying to explain to God what she had been experiencing. Sydney asked God for His divine wisdom and to reveal the underlining meaning of the dreams:

The bad dreams started when I was five years old. I can recall being at home, in a deep sleep, during a weekend sleepover with my cousins Sasha, who was seven years old, and Melba, who was five years old. It was just a typical weekend full of fun and playing games together as usual. I loved the weekends because my mulatto cousins would always come over and spend the night. Sasha and Melba were my "favorite cousins," and they both were so beautiful. Their skin tone was very light, and they both had beautiful long wavy hair.

Because we were such young kids, out of curiosity, we would always try to understand why they were so light and why I was so dark. It was a mystery to us for years. Of course, they never knew about their mother's secret past life as a working woman, nor did they know that their biological father was a Caucasian man. They were always told that their father was a black man named Nick. So, since the parents they've always known had dark skin just like mine (despite Sasha and Melba being extremely light), their heritage remains to this day a mystery. They both still believe that they are not mixed and that they have two African American parents.

I can remember Melba would always fall asleep first while Sasha and I would chat about our dreams and boys. Sasha would then fall asleep shortly after Melba. On this one night, I fell into a deep sleep. I can't remember the full details of the dream, but what I can remember has stuck with me for a lifetime.

In my dream, a huge red snake was slithering its way on top of my bed, trying to kill me and then eat me. In the dream, everything felt real. I was trying to get away from the snake, but I was stuck. It was like I was paralyzed from the waist down because my legs couldn't move. The dream seemed so real. I began to scream for my life. As the tears fell down my face, my father rushed into my bedroom to save me from the big red snake. The

Chapter 8: Dreams of Death

snake was real in my mind, and in the dream, the snake was trying to take my life. Before the snake could kill me, my father turned on the light to comfort me and assure me that everything was ok. Still, I was convinced that the red blanket on my bed was a venomous serpent.

Another recurring dream that I have had is one where I am hiding behind a large sofa to dodge gunfire and random bullets that never stop. Men are shooting at me, and I am always praying and asking God to save me. Instantly before the men kill me or before they would find me, I would always wake up.

Sometimes in the dreams, I am screaming for help or running for my life, and no one ever helps me or saves me. Frequently I am struggling to wake up but somehow manage to break myself from the exhausting encounter of events that happens during the dreams.

As I reflect upon the bad dreams, I can't help but mention that my daughter has had many bad dreams as well. Often, in the middle of the night, I am awakened by the sound of her crying in her sleep. Each time I ask her to tell me about her dreams, she tells me that the bad guys take me away, and she can never see me again.

Another dream that she has had was that the bad guys break into our home; they take all our things, and then they take me away.

As Sydney's body appeared to lay lifelessly in the pearly white casket, the soul and spirit within her give her the ability to communicate with God. Sydney was able to pray a poem to her creator. Sydney believed that the Almighty God could hear her poem-like prayer and that God could save her from eternal hell.

Lord I've made up my mind, this time I'm living for you.

For I have traveled through storms and Lord I know that it's you.

The One who won't let me down or let me get in the way.

Of your path and your plans, sometimes I don't understand.

How can your love and your grace erase the tears from my face?

From the pain of my shame, shadows of the past remain.

Weighing heavy deep on my brain, stuck to the core of my frame.

Chapter 8: Dreams of Death

Lord I'm crying out now, please Lord don't let me down.

SYDNEY'S BLEU

Chapter 9: Lust and Deception

Emanuel, one of Syd's male friends, introduced her to Buck. Buck played professional football for the NFL, on the Atlanta team. Buck was a typical jock: tall, dark, and handsome. Buck's complexion resembled a lovely shade of sun-kissed bronze. Buck's teeth were beautifully aligned, straight, and as perfect as they come. His smile was like a ray of sunshine. His physique was muscular; two hundred and ten pounds of perfection. Buck had a six-pack and then some. Buck's stature was built beautifully, kind of like a Greek warrior.

Buck swept Syd off her feet the minute she met him. When Emanuel called Syd on the phone and invited her to have lunch with him and Buck, he said, "Sydney, I want you to come meet my homeboy. He just moved here from Texas." Syd replied, "Okay, text me the address of where you're at, and I'll be there in an hour. I have to finish my client's hair." Syd didn't mind meeting Emanuel for lunch because he always cracked jokes, and he was always lots of fun to hang out with. Syd did not have many girlfriends, so Emanuel was the closest person that she would consider as a friend.

When Syd arrived at the five-star restaurant, Buck instantly mesmerized her. Emanuel grinned while introducing them, "Sydney, this is my partner Buck. Buck, this is Sydney." As Syd sat down, her heart began to thump. Buck's hazel-brown eyes remained fixated on Syd. His stature and body language made her nervous; she began to have an anxiety attack. Syd quickly excused herself from the dinner table. "Guys, I have to go to the restroom," she stated. All eyes were focused on Syd as she prayed to God, "Lord, please don't let me fall on the way to the bathroom," she said quietly under her breath. While in the restroom, Syd stared in the mirror to check her face and readjust her hair. She had to make sure that she was on point. As Syd primped herself in front of the mirror, she said to herself, "If I had known how

Chapter 9: Lust and Deception

attractive Buck was, I would have stopped at home first before showing up at this restaurant.

While walking back to the table, she noticed Buck staring at her from head to toe. The chemistry between them was definitely lust-at-first sight. Syd wanted that man just as bad as he wanted her, but she was thinking about marriage and starting a family with him. She was so shallow at that moment. All she could think about was waking up each morning of her life and seeing Buck's Zeus-like body and his adorable face.

Buck and Syd began to engage in small talk. She was elated and could not stop blushing. The entire time, Syd fantasized about what it would be like to kiss Buck's thick juicy lips. His teeth were perfectly white, and all Syd could see and hear were his lips and teeth saying, "Sydney, I want you!" Buck looked like marriage material, the kind of man that you introduce to your grandparents. Buck had sex appeal, swagger, and confidence. He was more than just a jock; Buck was also educated. He completed four years of college before being drafted into the NFL. He was the type of man that all women could appreciate. While sitting near Buck,

Syd's sacred parts became unusually moist at the thought of him.

After having lunch, with Emanuel and Buck, Syd drove back to the beauty salon. Her cellphone rang several times before she could get out of her car. It was Buck on the other end. "Sydney, what are you doing tonight, this is Buck." "I'll be at the salon until eight. I have a couple more clients to take care of," Syd answered. "I want to see you again," Buck said. "Me too," Syd thought to herself but held back, then said, "I'll have some time next week." "I can't wait that long. Why don't you come over tonight, and I'll make you dinner," he pleaded with Syd, but she was playing hard to get. She wanted to spend time with Buck so bad, but she managed to resist. Syd replied, "My client just walked in. Call me back around eight o'clock, ok?"

At seven fifty-seven on the dot, Syd's phone rang. It was Buck insisting that she come over and have dinner with him. "Buck, I'm still working, I had two more clients come in. Tonight is not a good night, and we just met. What's the rush? I'll hook up with you soon." In his smooth sexy voice, he asked Syd to call

Chapter 9: Lust and Deception

him when she finished at work. Still trying to play hard to get, Syd did not call him back that evening. She fought the temptation even though she was totally feeling him. Syd's mind and body were saying "yes," but the fear of God helped her to temporarily hold back her desires for Buck.

The next morning within ten minutes of arriving at work, a courier walked into the salon with a package. Stacey, the salon owner, signed for the delivery, read the label, walked over to Sydney with a smile on her face, and handed her the package. Syd opened the box, and it was two dozen long stem red roses. The package also contained a note. It read, "Sydney, please have dinner with me tonight at my house. My address is 4248 Country Club, Dr. Flowery Branch, Georgia. I'm looking forward to seeing you, Buck." "Oh my God," Syd thought, "This man is feeling me." Stacey and the other stylists complimented and admired how beautiful the roses were. They also probed and questioned Sydney about who sent them.

Buck called Sydney five different times that day, each time, she ignored his calls because she was too busy with clients. Syd really did like Buck, but she was playing games. Syd didn't want to seem too available or too easy, so she continued to play hard to get. A whole day had passed by without Syd talking to him. The next morning, she called Buck to thank him for the roses. He expressed again how much he wanted to spend time with Syd. So, she agreed to meet with him that weekend. He asked Syd, "Can you take the whole weekend off? I want to show you something that I think you might like." "I'll think about it," Syd replied.

   Saturday night, after Syd finished all her clients for the day, she drove to Buck's house. Syd was shocked that Buck lived within a gated community inside an elegant country club. As she pulled up to the entrance of the country club, the security guard asked her name, wrote down Syd's license plate number, and then called Buck. After confirming with Buck about his expected guest, the security guard allowed Syd access into the private community. Millions of thoughts ran through Syd's mind as she drove around looking for house number 4248. "What am I doing here? Why am I doing this? I don't even know this man." Syd finally pulled

Chapter 9: Lust and Deception

into Buck's driveway; instead of parking the car, she shifted gears, went into reverse, and began to back out. Then she changed her mind and shifted the gear back into drive. Syd drove her car completely into Buck's driveway, got out the car, then walked up to his home and rang the doorbell. When Buck answered the door, Syd almost fainted. Her heart felt like it was about to explode. She had played hard to get long enough.

    Buck embraced Syd's body for at least two minutes without letting go; he gave her the kind of hug you give to someone that you really love or hadn't seen in a very long time. After the long bear-hug, he escorted Syd to the kitchen. Her mind was so lost into Buck that she didn't pay any attention to how beautiful his home was. Syd did notice how Buck set the mood for a night full of romance. Twelve thick white candles were lit and burnt the scent of rosemary throughout the home. There were two round wine glasses half-filled with Merlot, and dinner for two was elegantly placed on the dining table. Buck prepared two thin cut steak filets, two baked potatoes, and spinach salad for him and Syd to share. This was the first time that any man had gone out of his way for Syd. Buck and Syd sat at the lovely prepared table and gazed into each other's eyes. After nibbling a bit and twirling her fork inside the salad, Syd had realized that she had finally met a real man, a man that knew how to treat a woman. Syd was head over hills about Buck. After playing around and barely eating any of the meal, Buck gently held Sydney's hand and led her upstairs into his bedroom. When they walked into his room and opened the door, there were red rose petals sprinkled everywhere, especially on his bed.

    Buck and Syd began to kiss, and they kissed some more. Buck led Syd to the master bathroom, where he had already prepared a bubble bath with candles. He enthusiastically started taking his clothes off, and then he stepped into the bathtub. Syd stood there in awe, staring at his body and thinking to herself, "What in the world is going on?" Buck grabbed Syd passionately and pulled her into the water. They both kissed each other with their eyes closed. Buck's body looked one hundred times better than what Syd had imagined. He had Sydney in his bath water with all her clothes on. The only thing she didn't have on was her shoes. Buck began caressing

Chapter 9: Lust and Deception

Syd's breast and putting his fingers in between her legs. Syd thought to herself, "It feels so good to be next to Buck, his body, and my body so close together." Everything was perfect, Buck had set the tone for an amazing evening full of romance, but Sydney still couldn't give in. She pulled away from him, got out of the bathtub, and abruptly left Buck's home in soaking wet clothes. While driving home, Syd said out loud, "I really like him, but who is he to think that I am some easy chick? A candlelight dinner, roses, and a bubble bath were not enough for me to give up my love to him."

Syd didn't talk to Buck for a whole week until he showed up at her job unexpected. All the stylists stopped what they were doing and stared as the superfine NFL football player walked over to Syd's salon station. "Sydney, what happened, why did you leave me? Can I talk to you outside?" Buck begged. Syd was totally embarrassed. Everyone in the salon was watching and listening. Syd started walking towards the front door of the salon, and Buck followed her. "I have two airplane tickets to Connecticut. There's a really nice resort I want to take you to. Sydney, baby, I can't stop thinking about you," Buck pleaded with Syd. Syd was already one hundred percent sold; she was buying whatever Buck was selling. She wanted to marry this man. Buck seemed sincere, so Syd agreed to go on the trip to Connecticut. Before they left Atlanta, Buck gave Syd three hundred dollars to give to her mother to babysit Rommel.

Buck drove Syd to the Atlanta airport. Syd blushed all the way there. She was clueless to the fact that Buck had purchased first-class seats for their flight. As they entered the plane, the airline stewardess looked at their boarding passes and greeted them by Buck's last name. "Hello, Mr. and Mrs. Armstrong. Thank you for flying first-class with us. We hope you have a relaxed and enjoyable flight. My name is Carla. It's my pleasure to serve you. Can I get you a beverage or anything before we take off?" the stewardess said with confidence. "I wish I were Mrs. Armstrong," Syd thought to herself. The flight to Connecticut was great; Syd didn't experience any turbulence. Just being with Buck was amazing; Syd felt comfortable spending quality time getting to know Buck. In the first-class section, all the alcoholic beverages were free. Syd and

Chapter 9: Lust and Deception

Buck were served a full course dinner while the other passengers were served peanuts.

The plane landed in Connecticut on time. As Buck and Syd headed towards the baggage claim area, they were greeted by a chauffeur from the Fox Woodland Casino Resort. The chauffeur had already stacked their luggage neatly on a luggage cart. The chauffeur walked directly towards Buck, shook his hand, and greeted him. "Hello, Mr. Armstrong, welcome back, Sir." From the moment they sat inside the limousine, Buck's hands were all over Syd. He sucked on her neck and caressed her breasts all the way to the resort. Syd was delighted with Buck's effort to impress her with the first-class flight and the limousine. Syd had decided in her heart and her mind that at some point during their trip, she was absolutely going to make love to Buck.

Finally, after a two-hour drive, passionate kissing and touching, Buck and Syd arrived at the Fox Woodland Casino Resort. The minute they stepped inside the resort, all the staff greeted Buck as if they had known him for years. "Hello, Mr. Armstrong. Welcome back Mr. Armstrong. Good to see you again, Mr.

Armstrong," people continued to repeat. It seemed as though Buck was a movie star. Syd wasn't a fan of football, and she had never really heard of Buck Armstrong, so she was kind of shocked by the attention he was receiving. The doorman of the resort took Syd and Buck's luggage to their room before they got there.

Buck suggested that he was going to spend some time in the casino, at the crap table. He handed Syd five hundred dollars so that she would have money to gamble. Syd stored the five-hundred-dollar bills into her small clutch purse then followed Buck to check out the casino. Without any luck, Syd played a few dollars on the slot machines. Ten minutes later, she walked over to the crap table where Buck was gambling. He had the look of defeat plastered on his face. When Syd approached him, he said, "I'm ready to go. I'm not having any luck today. I just lost fifteen thousand dollars. We'll come back in the morning". Nonchalantly they left the casino and headed back to their hotel room.

"Oh my God," Syd thought as they entered the hotel room, which was the presidential suite. This room was like nothing Syd had ever seen before. The rate for

Chapter 9: Lust and Deception

the room was normally fifty-five hundred dollars per night, but Buck was given the place for free because he was one of the casino's high rollers. The presidential suite was a perk given to high rollers who frequently gambled at the casino/resort. The room was five thousand square feet and included a butler. The floors were marble throughout the room. It had two spiral stairwells that led to the master bedroom. Inside the master bathroom, from ceiling to floor, all the walls were made of mirror. The bathtub was made of twenty-four karat gold. The toilet and the floors were electronically heated, and motion censored. The room was immaculate. Syd thought that she had died and gone to "Rich-folks heaven."

"Buck, this place is wonderful. I love it. It's beautiful here," Syd mentioned to Buck with excitement in her voice. "Sydney, baby, this is nothing. This is just the beginning," Buck replied. With his smooth sexy voice, Buck said, "Come here Sydney." He reached for the chocolate covered strawberries and fed them to Syd one bite at a time. This was the absolute most romantic experience that Syd had ever experienced in her life.

Buck picked Syd up and carried her into the bedroom. He removed all her clothes one piece at a time. First, he lifted her top, then removed her jeans. Buck took his time seducing her. As Syd was lying on the bed, Buck rubbed and massaged her body from head to toe. Not only did he use his hands, he used his tongue. Buck sucked and licked every part of Syd's body. Buck picked her up again and carried her into the bathroom. With his gentle hands, he laid Syd into the golden bathtub. He continued to kiss her lips and feed her chocolate covered strawberries.

    The bathwater felt good, but it was even better when Buck joined Syd. He asked Syd to stand up, so she did. He said that he wanted to do something to Syd only if she promised not to scream. Curiously Syd asked, "What do you want to do?" Buck said, "Close your eyes." So, Syd did exactly what he asked. She closed her eyes. Buck grabbed Syd's naked body and began to spray both of their bodies with cold water. It was shocking yet refreshing at the same time. The cold water splashing onto Syd's body felt quite amazing to her. Syd enjoyed the excitement and new experiences. Buck knew

Chapter 9: Lust and Deception

exactly what to do and how to do it. As he kissed Syd's neck, he passionately asked, "Sydney, please make love to me. I want you so bad." Buck slowly kissed Syd from her neck down to the rest of her body. Buck got down on one knee then lifted Syd's legs onto his shoulders. He engaged himself into all Syd's body parts until she begged him to stop. The intimacy started in the bathtub, then moved to the bathroom countertop, then onto the bed. In Syd's mind, making love to Buck was fascinating because Syd was so infatuated by his looks. Syd put her all into the moment; she gave Buck all her passion. Syd wanted to please Buck in any way that she could. His package down there was neither big nor small. It was just ok, yet he knew what to do with what he had. More than anything, Syd enjoyed looking at his body. Syd was sprung; Buck had Syd in the palm of his hand.

They made love in the limousine on their way back to the airport. Buck really did it for Syd; she was super attracted and turned on by Buck Armstrong. Their relationship went on like this for one year. After their third trip to the Fox Woodland Casino Resort, Buck gave Syd the keys to his home, his garage door opener, and the security code to come and go as she pleased. Buck really liked Syd, and he expressed to Syd that she was the one for him. "My prince has finally found me," Syd would say to herself concerning her relationship with Buck. She was almost positive that they would get married. All the right signs were there. Their relationship had chemistry and trust. Syd was devoted and dedicated to Buck.

    Out of nowhere, Emanuel telephoned Syd. "Sydney, what's up? How are you? I haven't talked to you in about a year," he said. "I'm fine. Thank you so much for introducing me to Buck! I'm so in love with him. He is the one. We've taken so many vacations together! We have so much in common," Syd replied. "Sydney, Buck just got traded to one of the NFL teams in California, and he is getting married next month," Emanuel said. Syd dropped the phone and tears rolled down her eyes for eight weeks straight. Syd called Buck every day for an entire month, but Buck never answered any of her calls. Finally, on his wedding day, he called Syd from a private number. She didn't answer because she never answered private or blocked phone calls. The

Chapter 9: Lust and Deception

call went straight to her voicemail. The words in Buck's message were, "Sydney, sorry I wasn't honest with you, and I'm truly sorry it had to end this way. Things just happened so fast. Today I'm getting ready to marry my high school sweetheart, the mother of my five children. Please forgive me and know that I never meant for things to happen this way, and please don't call me again."

Syd's heart was broken into one thousand pieces…she really loved Buck.

SYDNEY'S BLEU

Chapter 10: Rollercoaster Gone Bad

When Sydney gave birth to her third child, Briana, things had gotten extremely bad between her and her husband, Vinny. Two months after Briana was born, Syd and Vinny had split up and were living in separate states. That's when she met James Bradshaw III, an investment broker for Merrill Lynch Stock Exchange. After his wife died in a fatal car crash, James contacted one of Syd's clients to obtain a reference on where to take his daughter for someone to manage her hair. Of course, Syd's client referred James to her. James Bradshaw III called Syd and set up an appointment for his daughter to have her hair styled. "Tuesday at one o'clock in the afternoon, I have an opening, see you and Missy then," Syd said to confirm James's daughter's appointment. James's voice sounded sincere as he thanked Syd for allowing him to make the appointment on such short notice.

Mr. Bradshaw and his daughter arrived fifteen minutes before their scheduled appointment. As they walked into Syd's salon, there was no eye contact between James and Syd. His daughter kindly introduced herself, "Hello, Ms. Sydney. I'm Missy. I'm here for my one o'clock appointment with you." Missy was very sharp and intellectual. "It's nice to meet you, Missy. I'll be with you in about ten minutes," Syd said kindly. Mr. Bradshaw and Missy took a seat and waited patiently for Syd to finish her client. Syd glanced at James out of the corner of her eye to see if he was checking her out, and he wasn't. To Syd's surprise, his focus was solely on Missy. Syd was attracted to him. "James must be at least ten years older than I," Syd thought.

Syd draped Missy and asked Mr. Bradshaw, "What would you like for me to do to your daughter's hair?" "I need somebody to take care of my daughter's hair. My wife just passed, and I don't know anything about hair. I would take her to the lady that did my wife's hair, but she's too far. Can't take my daughter out

Chapter 10: Rollercoaster Gone Bad

to Buckhead to get her hair done, it's too long of a drive. I need somebody closer to home, so Tina, my wife's friend, referred us to you." "Ok, I'll take care of your hair, Missy. Mr. Bradshaw, she's in good hands. If you like, you can go and run some errands. I'll probably be finished in about one hour and thirty minutes," Syd said. "Perfect, I'll be back here around three o'clock," James replied.

Five minutes to three o'clock, Mr. Bradshaw walked through the salon door, smiling and grinning at his daughter. He complemented Missy on how beautiful her hair was and told her how pretty she looked. His reaction to his daughter reminded Syd of the deep love that Syd had shared with her own father.

Every appointment Mr. Bradshaw scheduled for his daughter was the same as the first. They always showed up on time. He would leave Missy with Syd, then come back to the salon full of compliments. They would smile at each other, the same way that Syd and her father smiled and grinned at each other when Syd was a child. Watching how Mr. Bradshaw treated his daughter was exactly how Syd remembered the good times of her relationship with her father.

As the months flew by, Syd secretly grew feelings in her heart for Mr. Bradshaw. Syd wanted him to treat her exactly the way he treated his daughter. Syd wanted him to walk into the salon and tell her how beautiful she was. Syd wanted him to put his arm around her and make her laugh too. Syd had a major crush on Mr. Bradshaw, and he had no clue. Syd was attracted to his walk. She was turned on by his confidence and intrigued by his smile. More than anything, Syd was attracted to him because he was a good father.

Syd secretly wished that Mr. Bradshaw would act like a father towards her, but he would never look at Syd to show any interest. With Syd, Mr. Bradshaw kept all interactions strictly business. He called Syd to set Missy's appointments, paid for the service, and kept it moving. Syd knew that he was a businessman because each time he dropped Missy off, he had on a suit and tie. Syd fantasized and wondered about what it would be like to date a businessman, not any businessman, just Mr. Bradshaw.

Chapter 10: Rollercoaster Gone Bad

On Thanksgiving Day, Mr. Bradshaw called Syd. She knew he wasn't calling to set an appointment because she had already done Missy's hair. "Hey Sydney, this is James, can you talk?" He said. "Mr. Bradshaw, hi, how are you?" Syd replied. "Sydney, you can call me James. How's your Thanksgiving?" he asked. "It's going fine, what's going on?" Syd questioned. "I just dropped Missy and my son Junior off at their grandmother's house. It's my first Thanksgiving without my wife. Sydney, I need someone to talk to. Can you meet me out, anywhere?" he asked. Syd heard the sincerity in his voice, and she knew he needed a shoulder to cry on. "I can meet you at Friendship Park," she replied with no hesitation.

Syd and James both arrived at the park twenty minutes after they hung up the phone. They got out of their cars at the same time, walked over to the bench and sat down next to each other. Syd noticed the sadness in his eyes, and he noticed the sadness in her eyes as well. James's eyes began to fill with tears as he reminisced about his deceased wife. Syd tried with all her heart to hold back her tears of sympathy for him. James poured out his heart more than Syd could handle. He told Syd about his deep love for his wife, their plans together, and how the loss of his wife has burdened his soul. "Why couldn't God take me?" he cried. Syd held James in her arms for hours, and that was the beginning of their friendship.

What started as a friendship quickly turned into a relationship. Each day, both Syd and James made it a point to go out of their way to see each other, sometimes two or three times per day. Each day, before going to work, James made morning visits to spend time with Syd. At least three times a week, he would bring lunch for Syd to the salon, and almost every night, they would meet somewhere just to talk. Syd helped James through the grieving process, and he helped her deal with the stressors of her life. They encouraged each other and gave each other support. They listened to each other's problems and cried on each other's shoulders. Syd wanted to be there for him in any way possible, and he expressed that he wanted to be there for her too. After a couple of months, their relationship escalated into a full-blown love affair. They could not hide the chemistry

Chapter 10: Rollercoaster Gone Bad

between them. They both were extremely attracted to each other, and they both always tried to impress one another. It seemed as if there was magic in the air whenever they were together. James made Syd feel so good about herself. Every day he would complement Syd; he noticed every single detail about her. James was the most attentive man that Syd had ever dated in her life. Syd was addicted to Mr. Bradshaw, a man that was almost fifteen years older than her. He was Syd's drug of choice.

The first time he came on to Syd, she tried to play hard to get. During their first make-out session, Syd abruptly pulled away, slid her jacket on then pushed her way out of his house. Syd's attempt to act like she didn't want to be intimate with him didn't work. After that day, they made love every day throughout their four-year relationship. Syd was one hundred percent committed to James. She wouldn't dare look twice at any other man except for him. James had Syd wrapped around his little finger. She couldn't get enough of Mr. Bradshaw. Every time they were together, Syd wanted more of his time.

She hated it when they had to depart or separate from one another.

The first year of Syd's relationship with Mr. Bradshaw was absolutely the best. The relationship was new. It was fun, and it was exciting. The second year of the relationship was excellent as well. They traveled to so many places and spent a lot of quality time together. The third year of their relationship took a slight turn from excellent to just ok. Syd was ready to get married, and James wasn't ready, which created a problem. During the fourth year of the relationship, Syd gave James an ultimatum, either he was going to marry her, or she was going to leave him. She planned to move away to another state or possibly out of the country.

At the beginning of their relationship, Syd and James started as friends, so the trust factor was there. They both opened up and spoke their hearts and their minds. The foundation of their relationship was based on trust and open lines of communication. They shared their goals and dreams with each other. They laughed and cried together. They came up with solutions and coping mechanisms on how to deal with their life challenges.

Chapter 10: Rollercoaster Gone Bad

James was exactly what Syd needed to survive the pains of divorce, and Syd was just what James needed to cope with the death of his wife.

The first year of the relationship was the best because the lines of communication were one-hundred percent open and because Syd and James made so much time for each other. They went out on dates every weekend. They did everything together; they were inseparable. They had a dynamic relationship, which included: roller skating, fishing, horseback riding, bowling, swimming, and jogging. They watched every movie that came out during their first year together, and they watched all their favorite movies from the past. Taking turns to cook dinner for each other almost every day became the norm, and if not, they would go out to dinner. They went to every five-star restaurant in Atlanta, from *Fogo De Chao* to *Ruth's Chris* to *Chops*. Each time they experienced a new restaurant, James made Syd try something new, and he would always order Syd's dinner for her. She liked that about him because no one had ever cared about her food choices, nor had anyone ever ordered her meals for her in the past. If

James ordered something that she didn't like, he would insist that the waiter took it back, then he would order something different. He also insisted that each meal had to be paired with the right wine. Their dinner bills were always around two hundred dollars, yet James never complained about the cost. He always said to Syd, "You are worth every dime I spend on you. Just you, being in your company is worth it."

They went dancing at least two times per month. Syd loved to go dancing with James because he had so much rhythm. They would dance the night away. He was such a great dancer that often there were times other women would ask Syd if it was ok for them to dance with James. Syd didn't mind James dancing with other women. She enjoyed watching him move on the dance floor. While he danced, it allowed Syd to see all the men that were checking her out.

James had season tickets to the Hawks basketball games, and Syd was his permanent date. James was very popular, so his friends and associates always invited him to different functions and get-togethers. Syd always accompanied him, and she would always blush as he

Chapter 10: Rollercoaster Gone Bad

introduced her to his friends. Syd loved to go anywhere with James. He was the life of the party and the center of attention.

The second year of their relationship Syd and James took lots of vacations. Their first vacation was to Maui. They stayed on the island for a week, but Syd didn't get to do much sight-seeing because James just wanted to stay in the hotel room and keep Syd on lockdown. He scheduled things for her to do while he was occupied. For example, he made arrangements for Syd to visit the spa while he played a few rounds of golf. She didn't get to visit any volcanos or experience any of the luaus. It was as if she was a prisoner on the Big Island.

Syd and James were often guests at Lake Oconee Reynolds, a Ritz Resort. There they would rent a twenty-four-foot pontoon boat and sail the lake all day. James would blast the music on the boat, and Syd would dance for him in her bikini. The dancing would turn into a striptease dance, which would end in wild intimacy. Syd loved that man so much. She would have done anything for James. Syd was so happy; therefore, all she wanted to do was make James happy in return. He loved to take Syd out on that pontoon boat. More than anything, he enjoyed watching Syd dance in her thongs and without her bikini top on. James was addicted to Syd. She livened up his life. Her perky breast and her innocent smile brought joy to his heart. Syd went out of her way to entertain James.

Syd and James frequently visited the high-end day spas. James would always book a couple's massage, so he and Syd could be in the same room together. When the massage was over, at the minute the massage therapists walked out of the treatment room, James would get on top of Syd to give her a sensual massage. He did it quickly enough not to get caught. He was a frisky older man, and Syd enjoyed every bit of it.

For Syd's thirtieth birthday, James planned a surprise for her. The week before Syd's birthday, he made her promise him that she would not schedule any appointments on her special day. On the morning of Syd's birthday, he sent a limousine to her home to pick her up. When Syd sat down inside of the stretch limo, she found a note that read, "Happy 30th Birthday

Chapter 10: Rollercoaster Gone Bad

Sweetie, I have a surprise waiting for you. I'll see you real soon. Love James Bradshaw III." Syd was mad that James was not in the limo, but she was super excited about the surprise. "Where are you taking me," Syd asked the driver. "I was told not to tell you. It's a surprise," the driver said with a smirky look on his face. It took about forty-seven minutes before they reached the undisclosed destination. The driver stopped, got out of the limo, and walked around to open Syd's door. When Syd stepped out of the limo, she looked around and noticed that she was in the middle of nowhere. Was this a joke, Syd thought? "Mr. Bradshaw is waiting for you over there," the driver pointed over to a building that appeared to be a large oversized garage.

    As Syd walked towards the building, she could see a large object that appeared to be a helicopter. "Oh my God, this is unbelievable," Syd said underneath her breath. James was standing inside the helicopter with one hand stretched out toward her. "Happy birthday, sweetie, you ready?" he asked with a massive grin perched on his lips. Syd was completely speechless; her lips were moving, but no words came out of her mouth.

Tears of joy filled her eyes and ran down her cheeks. Syd was surprised. "I figured since you're not in your twenties anymore, you should see the world from a different view. The sky is the limit Sydney, and I want to take you there." The pilot waited for Syd to step inside the helicopter before he securely closed the door. Syd was in heaven. No man had done anything like this for her. Buck had flown Sydney first class, but that was no comparison to flying in a private helicopter. Syd was outdone. She was literally and physically on cloud nine.

While flying over Atlanta for hours, James placed a little box in Syd's hand. "Open it, Sydney, it's not a ring, but it's something that I hope you will like," he said. Syd took her time and opened it slowly. Inside the box was a sparkling two karat diamond bangle. Although she was expecting a diamond engagement ring, she was very pleased with the bangle. As James put the bangle on Syd's wrist, he stared into her eyes and asked, "You like it, sweetie?" Syd nodded her head and answered, "Yes, I love it. I love you. James, you didn't have to do all of this for me." "Sweetie, you deserve more. You are an amazing woman, Sydney." They

Chapter 10: Rollercoaster Gone Bad

kissed, which led to touching, which led to James grinding on top of Sydney. He sucked and caressed every inch of Syd's body. He begged Syd to pull her underwear down. "I just want to feel you, Sydney please let me touch it." He touched it then put his face down in between her thighs.

During their third year of dating, things changed. They both were obsessed with each other. James wanted to control Syd, and she tried to control him. James wanted to go out with his friends, yet he insisted that Syd had to stay at home. Syd wanted James to marry her; she was worried about him going out and meeting someone else. Eventually, their relationship turned into a love-hate situation. Syd refused to sit at home while James went out and partied with his friends. He would curse Syd out every time he found out that she went to the club with her friends instead of staying in the house and waiting for him. Syd dated James for three years and still didn't have a ring on her finger. This was the longest relationship she had ever been in. Every time Syd and James spent quality time together, she would drop hints to suggest that she was ready to take their relationship to the next level. Syd thought that he was ready too because when she mentioned her desire for a ring, he asked her to meet him at the mall, so he could get an idea of what type of ring she liked.

    Window shopping for a ring started out as a wonderful experience. They both picked out different styles and different designs of rings. James's taste and sense of style were simple. He had predetermined the exact price range that he was willing to spend for Sydney's engagement ring. Syd wanted a two-karat diamond ring, but she wanted it to be different. James's budget and mentality were that Syd could have anything under three-thousand dollars. The problem was that every ring Syd liked was priced at over six-thousand dollars. Syd wanted something on her finger that she would love to look at for the rest of her life. Syd didn't want to get a mediocre ring that was just ok.

    For months Syd and James went to over fifty different jewelry stores. Ring shopping turned into a very stressful and draining experience. Sometimes Syd and James would argue inside the jewelry stores, and he would walk out yelling, "Eleven-thousand dollars, you

Chapter 10: Rollercoaster Gone Bad

must be out of your damn mind. I'm not spending that kind of money on a ring." Syd would be so embarrassed, standing in the jewelry store by herself, after he stormed out the door. James had spent thousands of dollars on her in the past. She didn't understand, why was he flipping out on her about the prices of the rings that she liked? James always told her, "Sydney, I want to make you happy. You deserve the finer things in life." The diamond bangle he purchased for Syd cost over twenty-five hundred dollars. Syd didn't get it, what was the big deal about him spending some money on an engagement ring? They would argue and go for days without speaking to each other because they couldn't come to an agreement about the ring. Finally, Syd gave up. "If I can't get the ring I want, let's just get a nice ring that has my birthstone in the center," she said in a humble voice. Syd picked out a ring that cost about two-hundred and twenty-five dollars. That was the day that James knew Syd wasn't in the relationship for the money. She wanted a two-karat diamond ring, but she settled for her birthstone because ring shopping was ruining their relationship. Syd didn't want to argue with James anymore, and she didn't want them to stop speaking to each other over a ring.

During year four of their relationship, the pressure was on. Syd was pissed off because James still had not popped the question. She desperately wanted to marry him, but he still was not ready. Syd gave him an ultimatum again, "You need to decide if this is what you want. I love you, and I want us to get married. What are you going to do? I've been your girlfriend for four years. I want to be your wife. We've been dating long enough for you to know what you want. Make your decision." "Sydney, why are you putting so much pressure on me?" James asked. "You know that I love you, and I want to spend the rest of my life with you. I'm just not ready to get married! My wife just died." "Your wife died five years ago, get out of my life!" Syd yelled as tears wailed in her eyes. She was fed up with the way their relationship was going; it was at a standstill. It was not moving, and she was determined to move on.

In an attempt to heal her broken heart, Syd closed her salon, boxed up all the things in her house, and relocated to Dallas, Texas. Apparently, she didn't move

Chapter 10: Rollercoaster Gone Bad

away far enough because James came to visit her every two weeks. He would fly and sometimes drive to Texas to spend time with Syd. "Sydney, come back home, baby I miss you more than you can imagine," he said during every visit. On his last visit to Dallas, James hired a moving company to pack all of Syd's things and bring everything back to Atlanta. While the men from the moving company loaded the truck, James and Syd headed to the airport. He had purchased tickets for Syd and him to travel to Miami. "Sydney, I know that you've been stressed, so I want you to relax. I have a business meeting in South Beach, and I want you to be there with me," he said.

The flight to Miami was about three hours long. After they landed, James rented a car and drove to a small building near the Miami Convention Center. "Sydney, I have to meet with my attorney to sign some paperwork. I won't be long. I'll be right inside there, in suite 22A. You're welcome to come in if you like," he said. Syd stayed in the car because she didn't feel like going in. Thirty minutes had passed by, then Syd got out of the car and walked into suite 22A.

"You must be Sydney, congratulations," the attorney said. James smiled as he handed Syd a key ring with two silver keys attached. Syd didn't know what was going on. James and the attorney shook hands, then he and Syd left. Once they got into the car, Syd asked, "What are the keys for?" "I'm about to show you, Sydney," James replied. Syd and James drove about two miles until they approached a small parking lot near the ocean. James got out of the car, came around to Syd's side, and opened the car door. He held Syd's hand as he helped her get out of the vehicle. "Turn around and close your eyes," James said. Syd did exactly what he told her to do. James wrapped a thin scarf around Syd's eyes and tied it in the back of her head. "What are you doing, you're messing up my hair!" Syd laughed with excitement. James bent down and eased Syd's sandals off, turned her around three times, held both of her hands, and made Syd walk backward. All she could feel was her feet tiptoeing backward in the sand. "What are you doing, James?" she asked. "I'm trying to make you the happiest woman in the world," he replied. James picked her up, held her body with both his hands then walked up some stairs. All

Chapter 10: Rollercoaster Gone Bad

Syd could do was scream. To stop Syd from screaming, James began to kiss her. "Sydney, tell me you love me," he asked and kissed her some more. "Yes, I love you," Syd replied. He finally let Syd down, then took the scarf off her eyes and said, "I bought this for us. Open the door." James had purchased a beachfront home for him and Syd. It was absolutely beautiful. The house was fully furnished, and the décor looked like something out of a Better Homes and Gardens magazine. James got down on one knee and asked the question that Syd had been waiting for, "Sydney, will you be Mrs. Bradshaw?" Syd had waited four long years for this day to happen. James held Syd's hand passionately as he slid a two-karat engagement ring on her finger. It was the very first ring that Syd had picked out when they began window shopping and searching for the perfect ring. He was the perfect man; James Bradshaw was Mr. Wonderful.

That evening Syd and James planned every detail of their wedding. They agreed that the wedding would be at their new beachfront home. Syd was super excited; she had finally gotten the man of her dreams. James was everything to Syd. James was her lover, her best friend, close like her brothers and just like her father. Syd's world was complete. Her man had finally proposed.

      Syd's mother and sister helped her to plan the details concerning her hairstyle and makeup for the wedding. Syd took no time to find a cute yet simple gown for the special day. The colors of Syd's wedding were silver and white. The wedding was small and intimate, only their close family and friends were invited. Syd and James said their vows standing with their feet in the sand facing the ocean. Syd's sister, Andi, was the maid of honor. Missy was the bridesmaid, and Briana was the flower girl. James's best man was his brother, Leroy. Junior, James's son, was his groom's man and the ring bearer. Syd's cousin, Melba, sang a beautiful old negro spiritual hymn at the wedding. As Syd walked down the aisle, she smiled and tried with all her might to hold back her tears. All eyes were focused on Syd, and her eyes were fixated on James. Syd and James exchanged their vows, then the ceremony ended. Leaving everyone behind, the newlyweds sailed away on a private yacht that James had rented. Syd felt like she

Chapter 10: Rollercoaster Gone Bad

was living in a fairy tale. This was the happiest moment of her life.

Syd and James sailed the ocean for two days. On the second day, as Syd rested peacefully, she was abruptly awakened by the tight grip of James's hand squeezing her face. His eyes were red, and he was furious. Syd felt her life flash before her eyes. James grabbed her neck with his other hand and choked her until she was almost unconscious. "You fucking bitch, I'm going to kill you. I saw how you looked at Leroy, and I know you want him!" James screamed at Syd. Then he let Syd's neck go. As Syd grasped to catch her breath, she cried: "What is wrong with you?" With his bare fists, James started punching Syd's face. She tried to block the punches and fought back to protect herself. Syd was fighting for her life. She tried to escape, but James grabbed her, took her toward the ledge of the yacht, then held her body over the railing, and in a rage, he threatened her saying, "Bitch, I will kill you." "Please, James, please, I'm sorry, please stop you are hurting me," Syd said, then instantly she fainted.

"Sydney, wake up. Sydney baby wake up. I need you, baby, wake up," James said. As Syd regained consciousness, James carried her back to the bed. Syd's fairytale turned into her worst nightmare. She couldn't believe this was happening to her. Surely, she was having a bad dream. Syd laid on the bed, bloody and bruised. Syd closed her eyes and prayed that she was just dreaming. When Syd woke up, she had realized that she wasn't dreaming. There was blood everywhere, and James was lying next to her, holding her securely. She tried to move, but she couldn't feel her body. James pulled her underwear down and got on top of her. He wiped the blood off Syd's face as he made love to her. Tears mixed with blood soaked the pillow sheets. He kissed Syd's lips and apologized, "Sydney, I don't know what came over me, I'm sorry. I'm so sorry I let this happen. I didn't mean to hurt you," he cried as he begged for her forgiveness.

As a child, Syd watched her mother go through the same thing that she had just experienced. Syd never in a million years thought that she would follow in her mother's footsteps. "Lord, I need you, please, Lord, I

Chapter 10: Rollercoaster Gone Bad

don't know what to do. James hurt me and almost killed me. Where do I go from here?" Syd prayed.

Syd and James went back to Atlanta and acted as if nothing had ever happened. Syd was still in love with him. Syd's friends and family brought gifts to their home and congratulated her and James. Mr. and Mrs. Bradshaw were the talk of the town. James traded in Syd's Honda for a brand-new convertible Jaguar. To make up for his violent outbreak, he transferred fifty thousand dollars into Syd's checking account. He and Syd never spoke about the violent incident ever again. It was as though it had never happened.

SYDNEY'S BLEU

Chapter 11: Europe Bound

On May 1, 2013, James and Sydney had an in-depth conversation concerning their relationship. James explained to Sydney that things between them weren't working out. With no warning or emotion, James coldly expressed to Sydney, "You need to move out of my house by the end of this month. I don't want to be with you anymore. It's over Syd." Sydney was quite shocked yet relieved when those words flowed freely out of James's mouth. She knew that she needed to leave their turbulent relationship but didn't have the courage to do so on her own. There was regular abuse that caused feelings to decline. She stayed out of fear of what he might do if she left on her own terms. So, when he ended the relationship, it was actually a blessing in disguise. However, she didn't know what she was going to do.

Sydney pondered on James's words and tried to pull herself together because she didn't have a plan; no plan A or plan B. Sydney's whole life was centered around James. Throughout all the drama that they had been through, Sydney had always forgiven James. They would always make up, and Sydney thought that she and James would always be together, forever.

Four days later, on May 5th, Sydney packed her suitcase and left James. Without any pre-planning, Sydney drove for one hour to Atlanta Hartsfield Jackson Airport with France on her mind. After Sydney parked her car and arrived at the international terminal, she walked up to the Delta ticketing counter. She politely asked the agent, "What time does your next flight to France depart, and how much is the fare?" The ticketing agent replied, "Where in France would you like to go? Paris, Lyon, Marseille?" Sydney answered, "It doesn't matter to me; whatever's the next flight." "A ticket to France is going to be expensive. There's a plane leaving here and heading to Nice in about an hour and forty-five minutes. You'll have a short layover in Paris and have to transfer planes to get to Nice. It's beautiful there, but the

Chapter 11: Europe Bound

cost for that flight is over twelve hundred dollars." Sydney responded, "I'll take it." Sydney didn't care about the cost of the flight, so she purchased a roundtrip plane ticket and was headed straight to the south of France.

Sydney desperately needed to go far away from James. She planned to start a new life as far away from James as possible. Sydney's goal was to go to France and find a job in a luxury spa or a high-end hair salon. She also had to find an apartment that she could afford. This was Sydney's big plan; start a new life across the globe, thousands of miles away from James.

The Delta flight over to Paris, France, was approximately eight hours long. Sydney had to switch planes and take a connecting flight because there were no direct flights to the south of France. When she arrived in Paris, at Charles de Gaulle Airport, she rushed and ran through the terminal to make it to the connecting flight to Nice on Air France.

The moment when Sydney found the correct departure gate, a beautiful French airline stewardess greeted her, "Bonjour Madame Sydney." "Oui, oui, bonne journée, merci, merci beaucoup," Sydney replied, trying very hard to speak in French. Sydney's three years of French language courses in high school were proving to be extremely helpful.

Prior to this particular visit to France, Sydney had the opportunity to travel to Paris a couple of times. Sydney liked Paris a lot, but she fell in love with the French Riviera, the southernmost part of France. Sydney loved, loved, loved so dearly the south of France. The first two times Sydney traveled to France, she was with her younger sister, Andi. Sydney respected Andi and gave Andi all the credit for pushing her to apply for a passport. Andi's very words were, "Syd, this world is huge. There is so much to see. You need to get a passport, so you can stop dreaming about traveling and just do it."

Sydney took her little sister's advice. She went to the local drugstore to have a passport photo taken, paid the necessary fees, then submitted the passport application and the other requirements. Sydney felt liberated when she received her United States passport in the mail. Sydney felt as though she had just received her

Chapter 11: Europe Bound

ticket to explore the world. The passport gave Sydney a sense of newfound life and newfound opportunity. With the passport, Sydney could travel around the world. Sydney felt like she had just become emancipated. Sydney had always talked about traveling abroad, but it was just talk before holding the passport in her hands.

EUROPEAN TRIP #1

London

    Andi strategically planned her and Sydney's first European trip. At that time, Andi had been living in Osaka, Japan, for at least a year. She worked at an international school, teaching English as a second language to Japanese school-aged children. Andi had traveled all over the world; therefore, she took the initiative to set up their first vacation in Europe.

    On their itinerary, Sydney and Andi's first stop was London, which was their meeting place. Andi was flying in from Osaka, and Sydney was flying in from Atlanta. After about ten hours on their separate flights, Sydney and Andi cheerfully met at London Heathrow

Airport. They hung out in Central London for three days. Thanks to Andi being so well rounded and well-traveled, she and Sydney were able to meet up with one of Andi's friends, Helena. Helena was originally from England, so it was awesome to meet with a native who welcomed them while they were on their first girls' trip in the United Kingdom. Helena joyfully showed Sydney and Andi around the tourist attractions in Central London. Helena was a great hostess for the sisters.

Helena and Andi did a lot of talking and catching up. Sydney was in admiration of Helena's beautiful British accent. Helena pronounced her words using great emphasis while using proper grammar along with the typical British accent. The tone of Helena's voice and dialect resembled that of a queen. Helena's attitude was bubbly as she was super excited to reconnect with Andi. They both taught English during Andi's first year abroad.

While Sydney and Andi were visiting London, Helena took them to some trendy little Irish pubs. Of course, they had to experience eating fish and chips, which is common in London. Sydney and Andi took

Chapter 11: Europe Bound

millions of photos while in London because they both thought that the vacation was a once in a lifetime trip. Sydney's favorite experience while in London was taking pictures of herself while standing in the historic red phone booths.

Barcelona

Next on the agenda was Barcelona, Spain. Andi chose to add Spain to the itinerary because she and Sydney both studied Spanish in high school. Unfortunately, they were not fluent in Spanish, but they thought it would be cool to visit a Spanish speaking country. They believed that it would be awesome to experience Spain and practice their Spanish speaking skills.

While in the aesthetically beautiful country of Spain, Andi and Sydney explored Barcelona via the city transit. They enjoyed sightseeing while relaxing on several local buses. During one of their daily excursions, they stumbled upon a beach, Platja de la Nova Icaria. After exploring the beach and the surrounding shops, Sydney and Andi visited a couple of quaint restaurants.

Andi and Sydney were able to enjoy a spa day at a cozy little salon. They both were pampered by receiving manicures and pedicures. Sydney wanted to experience several other services but couldn't because all the other services were too expensive and outside of the small budget that Sydney allocated for her first European trip.

Barcelona was beautiful, but Sydney and Andi were somewhat disappointed because they both couldn't communicate with the people. The Spanish language that they had learned in the United States was very different than the Spanish spoken in Spain. Sydney and Andi stayed in Barcelona for three days; then, they traveled to Milan, Italy.

Milan

All that Sydney could say or think of pertaining to Italy was, "Oh my God, the Italian men are so hot." There were so many drop-dead gorgeous men in Italy. From Sydney's experience, the Italian men were extremely attracted to women with brown skin. When she and Andi arrived in Milan, Sydney felt a little

Chapter 11: Europe Bound

uncomfortable while in that country. The men were so attractive, and the men were so attracted to Sydney. Sydney felt like all eyes were on her every single minute of her stay in Milan. She confided in Andi, "This may seem weird, but I felt like the Italian men want my body and my blood."

During their stay in Italy, Sydney and Andi rented a room at the Hilton Hotel located in the heart of Milan. On their second day in Italy, Andi was determined to go shopping at the Duomo di Milano. Sydney wasn't interested in going shopping. She wanted to visit the local beauty salons and spas so that she could take pictures and get an idea of the similarities and the differences of the beauty industry in Italy. Sydney and Andi decided to go their separate ways for that day.

Sydney left the hotel room with the intent of discovering facts about Italy's beauty industry. Instead, Sydney somehow fell into a situation with a tall, dark, and handsome Italian stallion. What happened to Sydney only happens in movies, not in real life, but this was real and not a dream.

As Sydney walked out of the Hilton hotel, she noticed that she didn't have her camera with her. As she proceeded to go back into the hotel, she saw a fine, well distinguished-looking gentleman staring intensely into her eyes. Sydney turned her head to look behind her to make sure the very attractive man wasn't looking at her. Sydney didn't see anyone behind her, so according to all the stares that she had been receiving, she knew that the polite looking man was checking her out.

Sydney was in awe at how well his body was built; his biceps, triceps, and deltoids were protruding out of his navy-blue Ralph Lauren polo shirt. Sydney was intrigued at how well the bone structure of his face made his appearance look flawless. His skin was smooth like a baby's skin. He had dark thick curly hair, and his light brown eyes complemented his entire Italian swag. Sydney walked towards the elevator, and ironically, he walked towards the elevator also. Sydney patiently waited for the lift, then all she could hear was a deep Italian voice saying, "Hi, I'm Paulo. Would you like to have a drink with me?" Sydney looked at the beautiful man and answered, "Sure, I'm surprised you asked, I

Chapter 11: Europe Bound

thought you were going to stare at me the entire time. I would love to have a drink with you."

Paulo's room was on the club level of the hotel, so Sydney went with him. On the club level, they had an unlimited amount of drinks and elegant appetizers. Sydney and Paulo had a great conversation full of flirting and making sexy eyes at each other. One thing led to another, and Sydney ended up in Paulo's hotel bed. This was the first time that Sydney had ever been alone with a man that was not American or of African descent. Sydney and Paulo played touchy-feely, and they kissed a little bit, but Sydney chickened out. She could not go all the way. Although Paulo was irresistible, Sydney was too afraid to cross that bridge. Sydney was not the type to have a one-night stand; she knew that she would never see Paulo again. Paulo was extremely understanding when Sydney interrupted their make-out session. She said to him, "Paulo, you are so good looking, I am very attracted to you, I'm sure you are used to women throwing themselves at you, but I just can't do this."

Paulo was extraordinarily passionate and a pure delight for the eyes. He was so handsome that Sydney had to take him back to her hotel room, so Andi could see how attractive he was. When Sydney walked into the room and introduced Paulo to Andi, Andi's voice uttered out, "oh my God, are you serious?" Andi was speechless as she stared at Paulo from head to toe. Andi was in a daze for at least five minutes. Both Andi and Sydney couldn't believe their eyes. It was unreal to meet a man who was a perfect ten. Paulo was the total package. After showing him off to Andi, Paulo assured Andi that he would show Sydney a good time while she was in his city. "Your beautiful sister, she will be safe with me," Paulo said as he smiled, showing all his perfectly white teeth. Andi smiled back at Paulo, then he and Sydney exited the hotel and began their search for Italian beauty salons and spas.

Sydney enjoyed a magnificent evening, holding hands and walking the streets of Milan with Paulo. As promised, Sydney was safe with the Italian stallion. He was nothing more than a gentleman who showed Sydney a fantastic time while in Milan. They ended their evening

Chapter 11: Europe Bound

over an authentic Italian pizza at a restaurant owned by one of Paulo's Italian friends.

Paris

The next day, Sydney and Andi caught a flight to Paris, France, which was the last stop on their itinerary. They saved the best for last. France was amazingly fun. When Sydney and Andi checked into the La Mercure Hotel, they were greeted by a handsome young mulatto Frenchman. He must have been ten years younger than Sydney. He smiled at Sydney with excitement in his eyes as he greeted her, "Bonjour Madame, comment ça va? Vous êtes américain? C'est un plaisir de vous rencontrer ?" Sydney replied with a friendly smile, "Oui. Je suis American." The Frenchman replied, "Je m'appelle Jean Pierre, et vous?" Sydney answered, "Je m'appelle Sydney et c'est ma sœur, elle s'appelle Andi. Nous avons des réservations dans cet hôtel. Pouvez -vous nous aider?" "Oui madame, J'ai votre réservation. J'ai besoin de voir votre passeport s'il vous plaît." Sydney rambled through her sack to dig out her passport then set the visa on the counter. After a quick glance at Sydney's

155

identification, the Frenchman enthusiastically said, "Voici la clé de votre chambre. J'espère que tout est excellent pendant votre séjour à Paris." Andi and Sydney began to laugh because they both could see that the young Frenchman had eyes for Sydney.

Five minutes after Sydney and Andi checked into their room, the telephone rang. It was Jean Pierre, the handsome young front desk agent, calling to see if Sydney and Andi wanted to go dancing later that evening. Sydney and Andi were excited to get an offer to go dancing from a local Frenchman, so they agreed to hang out with him.

Later that evening, around ten o'clock, Sydney and Andi got dressed then they met Jean Pierre in the hotel lobby. Jean Pierre called a yellow cab to take them to a hip nightclub. When they arrived at the nightclub, Jean Pierre led them through a dark alley to get into the back entrance of the underground club. They had to walk down a flight of stairs before going into the dungeon-like night club. It seemed like they had to go through a maze to finally get to the part of the club where people were. Once in the club, the music blasted, the club was packed, and Sydney enjoyed experiencing French nightlife. Sydney danced all night long. Jean Pierre wanted to smile in Sydney's face for the entire evening, but after about two hours, Sydney was tired of him. She wanted to talk to some other guys. Jean Pierre was really handsome, but when he and Sydney were dancing, she was not feeling him at all. Jean Pierre danced kind of like a girl. He was twisting and shaking his behind and hips a little bit too much for Sydney.

    Andi stood near the bar, cracking up, laughing the entire time while Sydney tried to ease away from Jean Pierre. Sydney was unsuccessful in her attempt to ditch Jean Pierre. As she inched away from him, he kept coming closer and closer to her. Eventually, she made her way to the bar where Andi was. She looked at Andi, and as they tried to hold in their laughter, they both began to crack up and laugh hysterically. Andi ordered Sydney a mixed drink. Sydney drank the entire cocktail in one swallow, and she begrudgingly tolerated Jean Pierre for the rest of the night. Although, Jean Pierre danced like a girl and was kind of clingy, Sydney and Andi had a great time.

The next morning after Sydney and Andi sobered up from a night full of French wine and dancing with French men; they went to see the Eiffel Tower, Notre Dame, and Arc de Triomphe. Andi and Sydney ate at several local French restaurants, and they took pictures in front of every bakery they passed. Most of the pastries in the bakeries were more like beautifully designed artwork delicately displayed as tantalizing dessert. Sydney indulged in tasting pastries and croissants several times throughout each day while they were in France. She and Andi couldn't help themselves; the deserts were extremely inviting. Sydney and Andi stayed in France for four lovely days then headed back to London Heathrow Airport. Andi managed to schedule their departures at the same time. She headed back to Japan, and Sydney came back to the United States.

Chapter 11: Europe Bound

EUROPEAN TRIP #2

South of France

One year later, Sydney and Andi planned their second European vacation. They met at London Heathrow Airport again. During the second visit to Europe, the itinerary included: Greece, Rome, Paris, Nice, and Cannes. The entire trip lasted for about twenty-one days. Sydney and Andi stayed two weeks in France because Sydney told Andi that she wanted to live in France, but she wasn't sure exactly where in France she wanted to live.

Sydney was enamored of France. She was intrigued by the French language, architecture, culture, and cuisine. Sydney also had a feeling that there was love in the air. In her opinion, the food was fantastic, and the men had romance written all over their faces. During this vacation, Sydney had her eyes set on Cannes or Nice (the southern parts of France). She was feeling the vibe of those two cities. Sydney could see herself fitting right into the French culture. She visualized herself working in an upscale French day spa and then eventually owning a small little boutique spa within walking distance of the Mediterranean Sea.

During the second European trip, while in the south of France, Sydney managed to find a little bit of time to do some exploring by herself. One morning, she left Andi in the hotel room and began her day with a brisk walk near the ocean. The scenery was breathtaking. As the sea sparkled, Sydney closed her eyes and inhaled every ounce of French air that could fill her lungs. At that moment, God reminded Sydney of the roads that she had once traveled. Small glimpses of the struggles that Sydney had overcome flashed right before her eyes. God spoke to Sydney, and he said, "My love, you can have anything in the world that you want. Just ask me, and I will provide it. Look at you, Sydney, you imagined and dreamed of traveling to Europe when you were a little girl. I brought you here not once but two times. You are not in Paris. You are in the south of France, a beautiful and luxurious hidden land." As Sydney jogged back to the hotel, she decided that she would pursue creating a life for herself in Cannes, France. When Sydney returned to the hotel room, she told Andi, "My mind is set on living in Cannes." Andi was indifferent, but she did express to Sydney that she liked the city of Nice more than Cannes.

Andi urged, "Syd, you should live in Nice. I like Nice. It's young and vibrant. Cannes is kind of stiff, and it reminds me of old money." Then Syd replied, "I want to be around old money. People with old money will be the target market for my spa. I can totally see myself opening a spa in Cannes. There are lots of tourists from all around the world here, and there are wealthy people here. Rich people go to the spa; they care about wellness and taking care of their bodies. Moving here would be perfect for business."

EUROPEAN TRIP # 3

Eze

James's comment about him wanting Sydney to move out of his house prompted Sydney to take her third journey back to France. This time she was physically and mentally alone. When Sydney arrived in Nice, the weather was absolutely fabulous. The sun was shining, and the temperature allowed Sydney to wear her pretty little summer dresses. With only one small suitcase, Sydney traveled from Nice to a beautiful medieval village called "Eze." Eze was calmly exotic and nestled at the hilltop of a mountain overlooking the coast.

    Sydney paid a cab driver sixty euros to take her to this hidden village. The fare was too expensive, but Sydney's experience in Eze was well worth it. Sydney stayed a few nights at a quaint little hotel in the heart of the village. Her room was within walking distance of Chateau Eza, the ocean, a famous perfumery, several boutiques, and a few restaurants. What Sydney liked most about Eze was the cobblestone pathways that lead into small caves. Inside of the caves were artists, painters, and craftsmen. The vendors within the caves were creating handmade items such as paintings, purses, and shoes, which were sold for forty to sixty euros and up.

    Sydney left Eze the next morning so that she could take a day trip, via the local bus, to Monaco and Monte Carlo. While waiting for the bus, Sydney met a brown-skinned girl from Madagascar. Her name was

Chapter 11: Europe Bound

quite difficult to pronounce. She repeated her name to Sydney three times, and Sydney still had trouble trying to remember it or say it. The girl from Madagascar looked like Sydney, and she happened to speak some English, so she and Sydney chatted until the bus came. Sydney told the girl about her plans for the day, and the girl explained to Sydney about her plans to meet with a friend in Monaco, which was perfect. The girl told Sydney that she was in France only temporarily because she was there studying at one of the top culinary schools in the world. She elaborated on her dreams of becoming a famous chef. She also discussed with Sydney about the difficulty and intensity of the culinary program. When she and Sydney arrived in Monaco, she met with her friend, but she also had time to show Sydney around before the two of them went their separate ways.

Sydney visited some salons and spas while hanging out in both cities. Sydney liked Monte Carlo and Monaco, but she knew for sure that she didn't want to reside there. After a busy day of exploring, Sydney took the bus back to Eze. When she arrived back into the village, she noticed a unique little restaurant. What caught Sydney's eyes were the Bentley and Ferrari cars parked in front. Sydney was somewhat curious about the restaurant and wanted to see what was going on inside. As Sydney walked into the elegant restaurant, she was greeted generously and graciously by a handsome male host. He had dark hair, dark eyes, and a sexy French accent. The ambiance of the restaurant was magnifique; that's French for magnificent. The restaurant resembled an indoor botanical garden. All the walls and the entire ceiling were covered with fresh flowers and greenery. The lights were dim, and the live music truly set the tone for a perfect evening while being alone in France.

  When the hostess brought a menu to Sydney's table, before she could look at it, Sydney knew that she couldn't afford to have dinner in that restaurant. When Sydney finally looked at the menu, she was ridiculously embarrassed. Sydney wanted to get up and leave, but she felt like she belonged in a place like that. The aesthetics in that restaurant were artistic and stimulating, so she decided to stay.

  The hostess came back to Sydney's table and asked, "Madame, êtes -vous en train de diner ce soir?" In

Chapter 11: Europe Bound

Sydney's most sophisticated French accent, she replied, "No pas de diner, maintenant, je voudrais mousse au chocolat et un café petit." Sydney ordered the two least expensive items on the menu, chocolate mousse, and a small coffee. Her bill was twenty euros ($22/US) for a child-size coffee and a small portion of chocolate mousse.

The live singer and musicians noticed Sydney enjoying the desert. After making their rounds to everyone's table, they came over to Sydney's table and sang the most romantic French song. Sydney had no clue of what they were singing about, but it was a moment that she would cherish for a lifetime. That evening Sydney had no date. She was alone in the restaurant. Still, the French singer, mandolin player, and banjo player made her feel as if they were passionately in love with her. As they sang French ballads to Sydney, everyone in the restaurant stared then clapped their hands when the trio finished their selection. Sydney just sat there and smiled the whole time.

The owner of the restaurant came to Sydney's table and introduced himself. He knew that Sydney was

American, so he was fascinated to speak with her. He showed Sydney a huge photo album with many photos of famous American celebrities, including Michael Jordan and Bill Clinton, to name a few. The owner was proud to have an American guest visiting his high-end restaurant. He and his staff provided superior customer service, and Sydney truly enjoyed herself that evening. After Sydney finished the last sip of her coffee and dessert, she reluctantly paid the bill. She thanked the restaurant owner and musicians, then headed back to her hotel.

Cannes

The next morning, Sydney's destination was Cannes. She took the bus to the train station in Nice then caught the first train to Cannes, home of the Cannes Film Festival. Cannes was exactly how Sydney remembered it; the same as the last time when she was there with Andi. Sydney was able to find reasonable accommodations for one night. She paid about forty euros to stay in a little family-owned bed and breakfast hotel within walking distance of the strip.

Chapter 11: Europe Bound

Cannes was full of fashion. It contained every luxury clothing designer this world has to offer. The restaurants in Cannes faced the ocean; the city is home to yachts upon yachts, upon more yachts. Yachts were everywhere. Cannes is a trendy tourist city. It's hip, and there's a lot of wealth. Best said, it's a vacation spot for people with money.

While enjoying a walk along the strip, Sydney glanced inside of a few spas. Two of her favorite spas were inside of luxury hotels: the Carlton Intercontinental Hotel and the Majestic Barrier. Those two spas were very classy, elegant, and on Sydney's radar. After checking out the different spas, Sydney walked into a posh little French restaurant. She ordered pasta, salad, and Coca-Cola. Sydney thoroughly enjoyed her meal, but she wished that all French restaurants would have more ice on hand. The French never put more than two or three ice cubes in her drinks. After she finished her meal, she people-watched for a few minutes then said to the waiter, "L'addition, s'il vous plait." The waiter laughed and said, "You speak good Spanish." Sydney had to laugh also. It was funny because she was trying hard to speak the small bit of French that she felt comfortable with saying. The waiter had a good sense of humor, so that made Sydney's day.

After eating, laughing, and making small talk with the waiter, Sydney was exhausted. She needed some solemn rest, so she strolled peacefully and slowly along the strip, taking it all in. Before Sydney could walk to the end of the street, an older gentleman approached her. With soft, kind words, he said, "Bonjour, madame, voulez-vous prendre un café avec moi." Sydney replied, "Bonjour, non, je ne parle français, je ne parle pas français." Sydney understood the word bonjour. Everything else the man said was a blur.

Sydney's French-speaking skills were good enough for her to order a meal and to ask for directions. She tried to listen and understand French when the natives spoke, but it seemed extremely fast and sometimes hard to follow. The French gentleman continuously asked Sydney questions in French. Finally, Sydney tried to speak French to him. The experience was quite humorous. Their brief exchange of Sydney's broken French turned into, "Oui, yes, I will have coffee

Chapter 11: Europe Bound

with you." Sydney cautiously agreed to have coffee with him. She figured that it probably took a lot of courage for him to ask a beautiful woman like herself if she wanted to have a drink with him. Thanks to modern technology, Sydney was able to use her smartphone to translate their entire conversation in French and English.

The Frenchman's name was Brand. He explained to Sydney that he was sixty years old. He told her that he was "un médicin" which means doctor in French. He said that he was married for thirty years and recently divorced for one year. He also mentioned that he had three children and two grandchildren. Syd explained to him via her broken French and with her American French accent that her primary purpose for visiting France was to find a job and an apartment. Sydney explained to him, "One day, in the near future, France will be my home. I want to start a life here in the South of France." Sydney told him about her travel plans while in his country, "Tomorrow I will travel to St. Tropez for one week." Sydney and Brand tried their best to communicate with each other for about an hour.

After sipping coffee and smiling at one another, they both made gestures suggesting that they were ready to end the evening and go their separate ways. Before retreating to her hotel room, Sydney and Brand took a long stroll around the city of Cannes. Sydney enjoyed talking and flirting with Brand. The hours began to drift away. Then by midnight, they finally arrived at Sydney's hotel. Brand embraced Sydney's body with a gentle yet passionate hug. He tried to kiss Sydney, but she turned away. It was too soon for all the mushy stuff, and Sydney still truly loved James.

Brand accepted Sydney's rejection concerning the kiss. Still, he intently asked if he could see her in the morning for breakfast. "Petit déjeuner, demain s'il vous plaît ? J'arriverai ici. Ici à l'hôtel à dix heures - ten hour." Sydney agreed to have breakfast with Brand. Sydney thought to herself, "He is cute for an older man, and he seems sincere."

Bright and early the next morning, Brand arrived at the hotel at nine-thirty. He called Sydney's hotel room from the lobby to let her know that he would be waiting patiently to see her. Because Brand was thirty minutes

Chapter 11: Europe Bound

early, Sydney was purposely thirty minutes late. Sydney's mother always said to her, "It's ok to make a man wait," so on this day, Sydney took her mother's advice. As Sydney fixed her hair and applied her makeup, the telephone rang again. In his lovely French voice, Brand asked, "S'il vous plait, je desire vous voir, c'est important." He was expressing his desire to see Sydney, and she was genuinely flattered by the French doctor. He was on time, persistent, and eager to see her.

    Finally, Sydney removed herself from the mirror. She put on her favorite pair of skinny blue jeans, slid into her cute black heels, and threw on her thin black sweater. For the finishing touch, she wrapped an exquisitely sophisticated golden scarf around her neck then quickly left her hotel room. As Sydney stepped out of the elevator and walked into the lobby, Brand just stood there and stared at Sydney. They both exchanged a warm and sincere "Bonjour," along with big hugs and huge smiles. Sydney and Brand embraced then set off for petit déjeuner, which is French for breakfast.

Napoule

Brand drove Sydney to a fancy restaurant in a nearby city called Napoule. The restaurant was high-class and offered a panoramic view of the coast. Because the weather was so fabulous, he and Sydney ate breakfast outside. There was romance flowing everywhere. Couples were cuddled up and sipping wine at eleven o'clock in the morning. It was a perfect day for lovers. Sydney enjoyed Brand's companionship. He was a quiet and soft-spoken gentleman. Brand opened every door for Sydney. Each time he spoke, he stared deeply into Sydney's eyes. He repeatedly told Sydney how beautiful she was and how her eyes were talking to him. Sydney was not sure what her eyes were saying because she was in deep thought about her relationship with James. During breakfast, Sydney tried to forget about her toxic relationship in Atlanta, but the entire time all she could think about was her relationship with James coming to an end after several years.

To show some interest in Brand, after they finished their breakfast, Sydney asked the waiter to take a photo of the two of them together. Brand was so delighted to be in Sydney's company, and Sydney was so delighted to have met such a kind and soft-spoken person. Compared to James, Brand was an angel sent to Sydney from heaven.

Mandelou

Brand suggested that he wouldn't mind driving Sydney to St. Tropez. Sydney rejected his offer and said no at first, but Brand insisted on taking her. He spoke softly, "Le plaisir est pour moi." He also insisted that Sydney allowed him to show her his home. Brand convincingly said, "La maison est très belle. S'il vous plait, aller avec moi." Nervously, Sydney agreed to see Brand's home, but in the back of her mind, she was kind of scared.

Sydney's mother always voiced her opinion about how she would never trust Caucasian men because of the terrible things that happened during slavery. Despite the negative thoughts that raced through Sydney's mind and the vivid images from the television series "*Roots*," Sydney accepted Brand's offer to visit his home. Before they began to travel through the mountains and up the hills of Mandelou, Sydney awkwardly asked Brand, "Can I see your driver's license. I want to send an email of your license to my family to let them know exactly where I am and who I am with?" Brand laughed, then showed Sydney both his driver's license and his doctor's license.

    Sydney and Brand traveled about forty-five minutes from Napoule to Mandelou. Brand's vacation home was uniquely situated high in the exclusively beautiful hills of the French Riviera. He and Sydney had to drive up and around a massive mountain before finally making it to the top. Brand's home was more than beautiful. His house looked like something that you would only see on TV. Everything about his mansion seemed surreal. The house was positioned near the very top of the mountain. The view from his home resembled the postcards that Sydney sent to her family while visiting France (during her first European vacation).

    As they pulled up to the entrance of Brand's home, he got out of his car to unlock the brown gated wooden doors that secured his property. He explained to Sydney that his father was also a doctor and that when

Chapter 11: Europe Bound

his father passed away, he inherited this home that his father built with his own hands. Sydney was impressed, but she also wondered if he was being honest with her. Sydney had been the receiver of so many lies from guys trying to impress her. She didn't know if she could believe what Brand was telling her, but he seemed sincere. Sydney thought to herself, "How likely was it for me, an African American woman to travel to the south of France and meet a single man that happens to be a French doctor?" Sydney wondered if Brand was really divorced. Their meeting was cute, casual, and comfortable, and there was no drama. It didn't seem real; the situation was just too good to be true. Sydney felt like she was living in a fairytale.

  What amazed Sydney most about Brand was that he was totally into her. He was super excited to meet a young beautiful American woman. Brand expressed to Sydney, "Vous rencontrer, c'est comme un rêve devenu réalité, car j'ai toujours espéré rencontrer une Américaine. Sydney, vous êtes le premier et le seul Américain que j'ai rencontré et à qui j'ai parlé." They both were excited about their encounter and their instant connection.

St. Tropez

After Brand gave Sydney the grand tour of his lovely home, he and Sydney left Mandelou then traveled to Sydney's original destination, St. Tropez. It took them about three hours to arrive at the highly anticipated vacation spot of the stars. St. Tropez had the reputation of being an exclusive exotic party town for wealthy people. Sydney wanted to visit St. Tropez for herself to find out what was all the hype about.

When Sydney and Brand arrived at the hotel resort, they collectively decided that they wanted to hang out together and see the island of St. Tropez. Instead of checking into the hotel, they went to a nearby port and took a ferry boat over to St. Tropez island. The boat ride was nice and breezy. Sydney couldn't control her hair from blowing in the rapid winds. There were six couples on the ferry boat, most of which were cuddled together and kissing. Sydney sensed that Brand wanted to kiss her, but she couldn't kiss him. Sydney just wanted to

Chapter 11: Europe Bound

enjoy his companionship, but she didn't want to engage in kissing with Brand. He asked Sydney, "Pour quoi, ne voulez-vous m'embrasser?" English translation: Why won't she kiss him? Sydney replied, "Je vous connais un jour, deux jours, pas de baiser, pas de baiser rapide." Translation: I know you for one day, two days, no kissing, no rapid kissing.

When Sydney and Brand reached the island of St. Tropez, she held onto Brand's arm throughout the entire duration of their day trip. Sydney felt comfortable with Brand, and it felt good to her to hold his hand. Back in Atlanta, James never wanted to hold Sydney's hand, so when Brand gently held her hand, he unknowingly reached a spot in Sydney's heart. Someone holding her hand was something that she had desired for years. While on the island, Sydney and Brand went window shopping in several little boutiques. To rest their legs and relax, they sat outside at a semi-fancy restaurant. As the sun began to set, they took the ferry boat back to the port then made their way back to the hotel.

When they arrived back at the hotel, the facility was completely dark. No hotel agent was standing at the front desk to greet them. There was only a handwritten sign on the main door of the hotel which said that the front office closed at six o'clock. This was completely insane. Sydney was stuck without a hotel room, and what upset her most was that she had previously prepaid for the hotel via a discounted hotel website.

    Brand and Sydney tried to contact the hotel booking company. They had no luck with their attempt to find a solution to their problem. Sydney finally reached the hotel operator. Still, the operator just continued to tell Sydney that she should have read the fine print on her hotel confirmation. Sydney was very frustrated about the situation. It was starting to get late, so she and Brand decided to go to a different hotel nearby because they needed to get some rest. They had planned to deal with the confusion from the other hotel first thing in the morning. Like a gentleman, Brand found a hotel and paid for their room for that night. The hotel seemed old, creepy, and deserted, but he and Sydney didn't have many choices at that time of the night.

Chapter 11: Europe Bound

After Brand paid for the room, the first thing that crossed Sydney's mind was that she hoped the hotel room had two beds. Sydney had no intention of sleeping with Brand. She had just met him. Hanging out with him and holding hands in St. Tropez was nice, but that didn't equate to Sydney wanting to sleep with him. "No, no, no," Syd thought to herself while she and Brand walked slowly to their hotel room.

They entered the room, and of course, there was only one small bed. Brand excitedly took his clothes off and hopped into the bed. He didn't take a shower or freshen up, which was a serious turn off because Sydney liked clean men. Brand and Sydney were out all day long and had a long drive. She couldn't believe that Brand was under the covers without first showering or bathing. He had the nerve to stare at Sydney with excitement in his eyes as if he had just won the lottery. "No way!" Sydney said under her breath as Brand stared at her like she was a piece of meat. In return, Sydney looked back at Brand like he had just lost his mind.

Sydney sat down on a rusty chair next to the desk. She was still in awe because the room had only one bed, and Brand was lying in it without first taking a shower. Sydney looked around the room then looked over at Brand again. She said to herself, "Hell no, this is not about to happen. I'm not going there with this man. I just met him and no. I will not sleep with him under these circumstances, maybe later on in life but not today, not now."

    Sydney calmly stayed seated on a seriously aged wooden chair. She had made up in her mind that the chair would be her imaginary bed for the night. While sitting on the uncomfortable chair, Sydney's eyes began to doze off. She was so tired, but she refused to get in bed with a man that she barely knew. Brand softly said, "Sydney, vous avez besoin de dormir." Translation: you need to sleep. Sydney wanted to sleep but not with him in the bed next to her. Sydney looked at Brand then rolled her eyes at him because she was disgusted. Two hours later, after she noticed that Brand was sound asleep, she quietly eased her way onto the bed. Sydney kept on all her clothes, including her shoes. She was really scared, so she prayed that Brand wouldn't try anything.

Chapter 11: Europe Bound

That morning, Sydney was gently awakened by the sound of birds whistling. She tried to slightly peek over her shoulder to see if Brand was still asleep. To Sydney's surprise, Brand was not in bed, and she noticed that she mysteriously had a blanket lying on top of her. She looked under the blanket to see if all her clothes were on, and they were, all except for her shoes. She figured that Brand must have taken her shoes off while she was asleep, yet her clothes were still on. Sydney looked around the room, but Brand was nowhere in sight. She checked in the bathroom, but he was not there. She opened the windows, looked outside, and didn't see him. At that point, Sydney began to worry. "Did he leave me at this hotel in the middle of France somewhere?" She said to herself. Sydney didn't even know the name of the town she was in, and she had no clue how to get back to the original hotel where she had reservations.

"This is some bull-crap. I can't believe this," Sydney said as she spoke her thoughts out loud. While she was saying a few choice bad words, Brand quietly opened the door and came back into the room. "Where have you been? I was worried. I thought you left me here!" Brand didn't understand one word that Sydney was saying. After angrily expressing her words, she noticed that Brand had breakfast for her in both of his hands.

Sydney was shocked and relieved. "Petite déjeuner, un croissant pour Sydney. Le sommeil, {the rest} is beautiful for you." Brand tried his best to speak English. Sydney was truly grateful for his thoughtfulness, and she was happy that he didn't leave her. In Sydney's past experiences, she had been left at hotels a couple of times. In Atlanta, James left her at a hotel simply because she upset him by asking him questions about his goals for their relationship. In the back of Sydney's mind, she remembered that day so clearly because she had to walk home in the rain that day. Sydney thanked God that Brand didn't leave her.

Sydney quickly showered and put her clothes on in the bathroom. She was kind of embarrassed because she didn't want Brand to see her without makeup on and without her clip-on half wig. Before Sydney came out of the shower, she pulled her hair up into a ponytail. She walked out of the bathroom, and when Brand looked at

Chapter 11: Europe Bound

her, he said, "cheveux - chicken, the hair resembles a chicken." Basically, he was saying that Sydney looked like a chicken head, and he asked, "What happened to your hair." Brand was fascinated by seeing Sydney's real hair. "Long cheveux hier, aujourd'hui cheveux courts." Translation: yesterday, long hair, today, short hair. Sydney's fake hair was an amazing discovery for him. Brand touched her hair and rubbed his fingers on her scalp. "Ok, that's enough," Sydney said. That wasn't enough for Brand. He pulled out his camera and took twelve pictures of Sydney, "Ok, that's enough. Let's go," Sydney said. She grabbed her breakfast, ate it quickly then they drove back to the original hotel where Sydney had reservations.

    When they arrived at the hotel, Sydney didn't allow the front desk agent to greet them. She began by expressing what happened last night when they arrived, and no one was at the hotel. Nonchalantly, the front desk agent said, "Sorry, we close at six o'clock." Then Sydney replied, "What kind of hotel closes at six o'clock?" The front desk agent nonchalantly apologized again.

Nevertheless, Sydney checked into the hotel, although she had a bad feeling about the room. She asked Brand to go with her to see the accommodations, so he agreed to look at the room. As they entered the empty room, Sydney noticed that there were no towels, no tissue, no sheets, nothing. She and Brand immediately went back to the front desk to make another complaint. The front desk agent replied, "The fee for towels and sheets is two hundred fifty euros per week." Sydney was disappointed about the accommodations, so she kindly told the agent, "Please check me out of this hotel, and please do not put any charges on my credit card."

As they walked back to Brand's car, he offered to let Sydney stay with him at his home in Mandelou, but he advised Sydney that he had to go back to his primary residence in Nancy, France when the week was over. Sydney decided that spending a week with Brand wouldn't be such a bad idea. She preferred to be with him in France than be alone for a week at a resort that had none of the basic necessities in the room.

Chapter 11: Europe Bound

Mandelou Round 2

The drive back to Mandelou took about four hours to complete. Sydney stayed with Brand for seven days after they left St. Tropez. She was comfortable with him. He prepared an early breakfast for her every morning. The view of France and the view of the Mediterranean Sea from his balcony was an extraordinary site to enjoy each day.

Some days, Sydney and Brand walked the streets of Mandelou holding hands. A few of their days together were just lazy days. They did nothing but try out different restaurants for dinner. They went grocery shopping together, and they cooked together. They went to a hair salon inside of a mall so that Brand could have his haircut. Everything about Brand screamed, "He's a keeper." He seemed so calm and positive. What Sydney admired most about him was his attentiveness. He spent an entire day helping her to recreate and translate her cover letter and resume to French. The documents that Sydney had were in English, with Brand's help, she stepped up her game and converted every sentence of her resume into grammatically correct French. Soon after, she and Brand went on a hunt to find a company that would print several hard copies of her resume. Their quest to have Sydney's resume printed was like a wild goose chase. As the hours passed by, and place after place did not offer printing services, they were lucky to find a small print shop capable of completing the task.

  Bright and early the next morning, Brand drove Sydney to Cannes and agreed to pick her up five hours later, which gave Sydney enough time to take care of business. Sydney was on a mission to land a job in France. She was determined to work in a spa or salon. Sydney dropped off her resume to five different spas. She didn't have any luck that morning, but later on, towards the afternoon, she came across a family-owned salon. The owner's name was Bernard, and his wife's name was Izabella. Bernard was from London, and he had a strong British accent. His wife Izabella, was an older Parisian woman. They both spoke excellent English, so Sydney was able to communicate her desire to work. Sydney expressed to the couple her plans of relocating to France. They cautioned Sydney, "It's quite difficult for an American to gain a work visa for France.

Chapter 11: Europe Bound

Citizens of the United Kingdom have a much better chance of obtaining a work visa for France. The government has rigid rules and regulations to keep the Americans out. To work in France legally could take you approximately twelve months up to three years. The French government will put you through many hoops and hurdles before you ever gain the right to work in this country. It won't be easy for you, but there are ways around the French government. You can work here with my wife," said Bernard. "The film festival is next week. You'll be very busy, but if you get caught working without a visa, you may be deported to the United States and never be granted access to return to France again. Come back Monday morning, and you can work if you desire to do so." Shortly after the meeting with Bernard and his wife, Syd took a brief stroll along the shore of the beautiful blue ocean. Syd had a lot to think about. She finally met up with Brand again and tried to explain to him about the spas that she visited and the couple that offered her a job.

Sydney and Brand's week with one another was coming to an end. On their last day together, Brand asked Sydney to go back to Nancy with him and consider spending the rest of her life with him. Sydney absolutely couldn't do that. She was in love with the south of France; she was not in love with Brand. His medical practice and home were in Nancy, a village located forty minutes away from Paris. Certainly, Sydney didn't want to live in Paris, and she wasn't too fond of the idea of living in a village, not unless it was the village, Eze, which happened to be in the south of France. That last day together, Sydney and Brand hugged and kissed. She finally felt comfortable kissing him, so she did just that.

Brand promised Sydney that he would love her forever, "My beautiful, young American woman, you changed my life forever. The love is true." Sydney believed Brand. She believed every French word that came out of his mouth. They exchanged their addresses and contact information and promised to write each other love letters. Sydney and Brand kissed one last time. He reluctantly got into his car and drove back to Nancy. Sydney casually walked away, then checked into a little hotel near the center of Cannes. Sydney and Brand didn't

Chapter 11: Europe Bound

have a teary-eyed goodbye. They had a goodbye full of possibilities.

On Monday morning at ten o'clock, Sydney was back at the spa and ready to work with Izabella. Sydney took her chances, yet she was extremely nervous. Sydney worked in the spa, although she didn't want to take the risk of being deported. Sydney worked on three clients; then, her conscience got the best of her. She told Bernard and Izabella that she was planning to go back to the United States to apply for a work visa. The couple agreed that Sydney was making the right decision. They promised Sydney, "When you return to France, you are always welcome to work with us."

Two days later, Sydney flew back home. She called James when she landed in Atlanta. She and James barely talked on the phone as she drove back to his house. They had forty minutes of silence between them. James had nothing to say and nor did Sydney. They both just held their phones and waited for each other to say something, but no words ever came out. By the time Sydney reached his house, he was backing out of the driveway. With straight faces and no smiles, Sydney and

James both looked at each other without any expressions or emotions. James drove off as Sydney pulled into the driveway. No hug, no kiss, no words, no more relationship, nothing. Sydney and James both knew that their relationship was over.

EUROPEAN TRIP # 4

Nancy, France

Three months later, August 26, 2013, Brand waited patiently for Sydney's arrival at Paris Charles de Gaulle airport. He didn't believe Sydney when she called him to tell him, "Guess what? I closed my business. I sold almost everything in the salon. I am moving to France. I hope your car can fit seven large suitcases." Sydney arrived in Paris after a long, turbulent eight-hour flight. She exited the terminal, passed through the international customs and security clearance, then made her way over to the baggage claim area. One of the baggage claim agents had kindly stacked all seven of her suitcases conveniently onto a roller cart.

Chapter 11: Europe Bound

Sydney pushed the roller cart for about two minutes; then, Brand walked right up to her. "Sydney," he said with a surprised expression on his face. "Brand," Sydney said with some hesitation in her voice. Something about Brand was different. He wasn't the same guy that Sydney had met a few months ago. His facial expressions seemed different. His demeanor was different. Brand's body language was also different. Sydney tried to remain normal in her approach, so she held back from asking too many questions.

Brand quickly pulled the cart, with Sydney's suitcases, to his car. He managed to load all seven of the large luggage into his vehicle with no problems at all. He sat down in the car, put on his seatbelt, and began to drive. "Where to, my Sydney," Brand asked. Sydney was not feeling good about Brand's strange demeanor. Sydney replied, "Let's find a church. I think the most important thing for me to do is to find a church. I did some research on American speaking churches in Paris. Here is the address of a church not too far from the airport." Brand looked at the address then proceeded to find the American Church of Paris. He knew his way around Paris, so he and Sydney arrived at the church rather quickly. "Aller Sydney, take your time. Je reste ici dans mon voiture."

Brand decided to stay in his car while Sydney went inside the cathedral. Fortunately for Sydney, the church was open. She walked inside to look around and to pray. She asked God, "Please be with me on this journey. I need you now more than I ever needed you before. I love you Lord, Amen." When she finished praying, one of the church members introduced herself to Sydney and invited her to come back to church service on Sunday morning. The church member promised Sydney that she wouldn't be disappointed. Sydney thanked her for the offer, then walked back outside to where Brand was patiently waiting for her.

They drove away from the church then headed to Brand's hometown, Nancy. Nancy was a small village with about two hundred inhabitants. Brand had an established medical practice there, so Nancy would always be his home. He wanted to show Sydney his home and his office, which, like his father, he had built with his own hands. He also wanted Sydney to consider

Chapter 11: Europe Bound

living with him, even though her mind was set on living in Cannes. She was ok with visiting Brand's home in the small village, but she was not ok with living there. Brand's home in Nancy was just as beautiful as his home in Mandelou. He had two enormous gardens full of gardenia flowers and a variety of vegetables. The gardens were surrounded by lush apple trees, orange trees, and pear trees.

  As they approached the entrance of Brand's home, he got out of his car to unlock the wooden gates, which were similar to the wooden barriers that secured his property in Mandelou. Looking from the outside at Brand's home, Sydney's first impression was, "Oh my, this man must be wealthy." Sydney noticed a large black and bronze metal marquee with Brand's name engraved in it. "Wow, this is where you live and practice medicine," she said. Seeing his name engraved next to the word médicin was Sydney's confirmation that Brand was exactly who he said he was.

  They entered Brand's home after a short walk through his garden. Sydney was in admiration of his lovely gardens, but she still had a strange feeling about him. Something about his demeanor didn't sit well with her. As she looked around Brand's home, he asked her, "La maison. Que pensez-vous? What do you think, Sydney, is my house good enough for you?" Sydney didn't reply to his question because she was intrigued by the stacks and stacks of sample-sized medicines that filled an entire wall near the living room area. "Why do you have so much medicine? Do you prescribe this medicine to your patients?" she asked. Sydney was confused about the abundance of sample packs of medicine everywhere.

  Some of the sample boxes were empty, which lead Sydney to believe that Brand was probably medicating himself. Brand replied, "The medicine companies send me many samples, and sometimes I have to try them out before I give them to my patients." Sydney was starting to become afraid because by looking at the empty sample packs of medicine; there was no telling what type of pills or drugs Brand was currently on. She kindly asked him, "Brand, which of these medicines are you taking?" He showed her three types of medicine that he took regularly. "I take this one

Chapter 11: Europe Bound

for the pain in my legs. I take this one to help with my depression, and I take this one to help me go to sleep at night," he popped two pills in his mouth as he responded to Sydney's question. "Dear God, what have I gotten myself into, please protect me," Sydney prayed quietly in a low voice.

Brand continued to show Sydney around his home. When they went up to the second level, he anxiously showed Sydney all his many paintings of nude women. Sydney was starting to get spooked out, but she had faith in God, and she knew that she would be ok. To show confidence, she calmly complemented Brand's artwork, "You drew this and painted all of those pieces of art?" "Yes, and it is my desire to make a painting of you, my Sydney," Brand stated, with the hopes that she would agree to allow him to paint a nude portrait of her. "No, I don't think so," Sydney replied as she began to walk back downstairs.

Brand followed Sydney back to the first level of his home. At that point, she was somewhat agitated and ready to leave. "Nice house Brand, can we leave now?" she asked out of desperation because she was totally annoyed. Brand got down on both of his knees and began to hug Sydney's legs. "Sydney, I desire to make love to you. The feeling is strong," he spoke with a strange intensity in his voice. Sydney's response was, "S'il vous plait, come on Brand. Let's go to Cannes. You know why I'm here. I told you that I was coming to France because I wanted to start my life in Cannes. Nous allons." Brand got up off his knees and walked out to his car. Sydney followed him and was relieved that he stopped begging her to make love.

    Brand didn't say a word as they drove to Mandelou. Sydney tried to ask him questions, but he continued to ignore her. After several attempts to engage in conversation, she gave up. They both sat in silence during the long-distance drive to the south of France. Each time Brand stopped to take a bathroom break or stopped to fill up his gas tank, Sydney noticed that he would put a small pill into his mouth. She remained quiet during the whole drive to Mandelou. Several hours later, they arrived at Brand's home in the mountains overlooking the seas of the south of France. As they walked into his house, Sydney had made a conscious

Chapter 11: Europe Bound

decision to call her mother. She wanted to let her mother know that she was currently in the south of France, but Sydney also wanted to inform her mother that there was something strange going on with Brand.

Sydney needed to talk to her mother in a code language, but it was impossible because Brand was staring at her and watching her every move. "Is everything alright? Are you ok? You must not be able to talk. He must be standing right there near you," Mom asked, yet she could sense that Brand was in her presence. "No. We just made it to Mandelou," Sydney said with a long-hesitated voice. "Call me back when you can talk," Sydney's mom said. "No, Mom, we can talk now," Sydney said desperately, trying to keep her mom on the phone. Sydney held the phone calmly without speaking a word to her mother, then suddenly Brand began to curse and yell in French. Sydney didn't understand one word that he was saying. He began to open and slam all the doors and windows of his home. Mom said, "What is going on? What is all that noise in the background?" "It's Brand yelling and going crazy, and I don't know why," Sydney replied. "I guess you need to get off the phone and talk to him but call me back in an hour so that I'll know you are okay," Mom said. "Ok Mom, love you," answered Sydney, then she calmly ended the phone call.

Sydney looked at Brand with an expression of disbelief on her face. She couldn't believe that he had thrown a temper tantrum while she was on the phone with her mother. "Avez-vous un problem, pourquoi vous angry avec moi?" she asked, trying to talk in French. Brand walked over to Sydney and aggressively put his hands around her throat. "Sydney, I have pain, I have pain. Vous no kiss me, no kiss me Sydney," Brand spoke anxiously while gripping Sydney's neck with both of his hands. Sydney couldn't speak a word because his hands were clasped against her windpipe. While gasping for air, Sydney almost stopped breathing. Finally, Brand let go of her neck. Then with both of his hands, he placed Sydney's hand near the crotch area of his pants. "How do I escape?" were the first thoughts that ran across Sydney's mind.

Sydney tried to walk towards the front door, but Brand grabbed her arm. "Désolé, désolé, pardon moi,

Chapter 11: Europe Bound

excuse moi, Sydney" Brand pleaded with her. "J'aller à d'hôtel, parceque je besoin de parler avec mes enfants, s'il vous plait," Sydney spoke calmly to Brand but deep down inside she was terrified and afraid of what he might do next. Sydney begged Brand to take her to a hotel so that she could call her children on Skype. He insisted that Sydney stayed with him, but she insisted that she needed to see her children and talk to them via Skype. Sydney had to say something that would allow her to leave his home.

Brand grabbed his jacket then dropped Sydney off at the nearest hotel. "Désolé, Sydney," were the final words she ever heard from Brand. Syd never saw him or spoke to him again. She wanted to stay as far away from craziness as possible.

Sydney was searching for something, but she couldn't find it because she had no clue of what she was desperately seeking. Was it love? Was it acceptance? Was it her purpose here on earth? Sydney's life was spiraling out of control. She was lost, confused, and had fallen off track both spiritually and mentally.

SYDNEY'S BLEU

♌ **12** ♌

Chapter 12: Haiti

For several months, Syd indulged in learning about the Caribbean island Hispaniola. She was interested in traveling to the Dominican Republic because she heard an ad on the radio about Punta Cana. Syd's standard pre-departure ritual was first to research a country before she'd visit. While researching Hispaniola, Syd learned that the Dominican Republic and Haiti shared the same island. She never learned about either country in grade school so, her findings of Hispaniola were intriguing. Syd enjoyed learning about both the Dominican Republic and Haiti, yet she was more interested in understanding Haiti's history, culture, economics, and politics.

Before Syd decided that she would go to Haiti instead of the Dominican Republic, she began to binge-watch documentaries about the country. She overindulged in reading published articles written by several historians concerning the truth about Haiti. Syd also searched the Internet to find historical landmarks to visit while in Haiti.

    Syd was fascinated to learn about the Haitian Revolution and Haiti's victory over the French, which ignited the abolition of slavery in the year 1804. She learned about the history of Haiti's heroes: Toussaint Louverture, Henri Christophe, and Jean Jacques Dessalines. Haiti's founding fathers led enslaved Africans in the revolt against the French, which ended slavery and helped Haiti to become the first independent black nation.

    Syd questioned the validity of the new information that she was learning because before researching facts about Haiti, she just believed the things that other people said about the country. The only information that she ever heard about Haiti was derogatory things concerning poverty and voodoo. Also, she knew that missionaries from all over the world,

Chapter 12: Haiti

including ministers from her church, would travel to Haiti to provide assistance to people in need.

When Syd was in her twenties, she secretly desired to be a missionary because she wanted to go to Haiti and Africa to help people. Her dream was shattered by the seasoned veteran missionaries at her church because, for Syd to become a missionary, she would have to take two years of missionary training. Syd started the missionary training classes, but she didn't complete them; she couldn't understand why she had to undergo so much training just to be a missionary. Within her mind and her heart, she was already a missionary. Syd prayed to God and studied the Bible. God's word was embedded in her heart, but the strict rules and regulations given by her church turned her away from continuing to want to do mission work.

On March 15, 2018, Syd finally lived out her dream of going to Haiti. Syd traveled there with her best friend from church, Andres Christophe Pierre. Mr. Christophe, as he was affectionately named, was an accomplished man who had studied at Harvard and finished at the top of his class. He and Syd met at church during a worship revival, then met regularly during their small group meetings. They became best friends because they had so much in common: they both loved to travel and visit new places. They both loved all types of food and music. They enjoyed dancing, and they valued family and education. They shared a love for the arts. They both were introverts and loved watching movies and documentaries. They enjoyed conversing and philosophizing about all things, and they had a mutual love and respect for each other.

    Mr. Christophe agreed to accompany Syd during her trip to Haiti. He was Haitian-American, born of Haitian parents who migrated to the United States in the '60s. He told Syd that he had many relatives in Haiti, so he was just as excited as Syd to visit the country. Mr. Christophe had only visited Haiti one time, but he promised Syd that he would be a great tour guide. What concerned Syd is that Mr. Christophe rarely spoke about Haiti. He often talked about his parents, but he never shared any of the history of Haiti with Syd. When she asked him questions about Toussaint Louverture, Henri Christophe, and Jean Jacques Dessalines, he didn't really

Chapter 12: Haiti

share the answers. Still, he would listen intently to what Syd had discovered.

When Syd shared information about Haiti's history and named places that she wanted to visit, Mr. Christophe seemed surprised that Syd found out so much about the country. Syd explained to him, "We have to see La Citadelle, in Cap Haitian. It's a historic mountaintop fortress built by Henri Christophe. Henri Christophe was a general in the Haitian Army who built the Citadelle to protect the new nation (Haiti) against attacks by the French."

Syd continued to explain, "We should visit some museums; there's Musée du Pantheon and Musée Ogier-Fombrun." "And, did you know that there are beach resorts in Haiti and waterfalls?" Syd questioned Mr. Christophe. He smiled and said, "My father used to always talk about a town called Jacmel and Bassin Bleu. Maybe we'll have the opportunity to visit those places. That would be great to see where my father grew up."

Mr. Christophe called several of his family members to discuss his upcoming travel plans. His family was so shocked that he was finally visiting Haiti.

It had been forty years since the last time he was in the country. Mr. Christophe's family members were so happy that he would be visiting them; they offered to have a driver meet him and Syd at the airport. His family on his mother's side agreed that they would host him and Syd in a rural village called Cazale. Mr. Christophe's family promised him that they would provide warm and welcoming accommodations.

Mr. Christophe explained the history of his mother's birthplace, where he and Syd would stay:

*"**During 1802 – 1803**, Napoleon sent Polish troops as a military legion to Haiti to help quell the slave rebellion.*

***In 1804**, A significant number of Polish troops defected from the French army and joined the slaves in the fight against the French. One of the troops supposedly was named Christophe, from whom my mother descends. Family legend states that Christophe was granted acres of land by Jean-Jacques Dessalines, the first president of the new Republic. The land, now known as Fond Blanc, was supposedly payment for supporting the slaves' revolution. Cazale is the fourth section of Fond Blanc,* which is a mountainous district within Cabaret, a town of Arcahaie.

In 1891, Jean Felix Christophe was born to François Christophe and Karine Silvain in Cazale. Jean Felix, affectionately known as "Jumba," was my mother's father.

In 1893, Marie Anne Mislen was born to Mislen Berline and Lisa Estille in Cazale. Marie Anne, affectionately known as "GanGan," was my mother's mother.

In 1933, Jean Felix and Marie Anne were officially married. Their marriage certificate declares that their six children should be legitimized by the marriage as if they were born after the wedding. These children were: Beatrice (19 years), Eunice (17 years), Jean Joseph (11 years), Patrick (4 years), Jean Paul (3 years), and Mica (1 year).

In 1935, Marie Louise Christophe was born to Jean Felix and Marie Anne. Louise was my mother.

January 1969, Louise left Haiti and family members in Cazale. She emigrated to the United States.

March 1969*, François Duvalier ordered the massacre of many residents of Cazale and commenced a campaign of terror and intimidation by his private army, the Tonton Macoute, that lasted several weeks. My uncle, Patrick Christophe (40 years at the time), was one of many men jailed as a result of this campaign.*

Syd was blown away by listening to Mr. Christophe's history lesson. "Why is this the first time I'm hearing this story?" Syd asked. "I told you about my parents, and I've told you several times about me having some Polish blood in my veins. Syd, you just don't listen when I tell you things," responded Mr. Christophe.

As Syd and Mr. Christophe planned their visit to Haiti, they both decided that they would pack light and only take backpacks with a few personal items and a change of clothes. Syd suggested that they take a few suitcases with clothing items to donate while there. She was happy to donate clothes to real people instead of donating to Goodwill.

Chapter 12: Haiti

HAITI DAY # 1

The flight over to Haiti was unique. From the sky, the view of the Atlantic Ocean heading into the Caribbean exuded a vast array of blues. The ocean's hues ranged from cyan to teal and turquoise blue, but as the flight got closer to the destination, the color scheme changed. Astonished by how close the mountains were to the clouds, Syd marveled at how the shadows from the clouds reflected onto each mountaintop casting the appearance of darkness onto all the mountains. The bottom of the mountains appeared to be a tannish-brownish color, but the tops of the mountains were a dark grey bluish tone. The view was dark and mysterious, yet it was magical because the mountains resembled an image created for a sci-fi movie; the scenery did not look real.

After the three-hour flight from Atlanta to Port au Prince, Syd and Mr. Christophe's adventure in Haiti began. They experienced some slight hustle and bustle exiting the terminal and getting cleared through customs. The customs agent scanned Syd and Mr. Christophe's passports, asked no questions, then allowed them to exit through the checkpoint to get to the baggage claim area. Syd was kind of upset when she finally retrieved her ravaged suitcase. All the clothing items which she had neatly organized had been scuffled through, and the zippers were broken. After reorganizing her luggage, Syd and Mr. Christophe began to walk outside the airport. Rhythmic sounds of live Haitian music gracefully acknowledged the travelers' arrival.

The driver, François, a relative and friend of Mr. Christophe's family greeted them in Creole and quickly escorted them to his van. When he noticed that Syd and Mr. Christophe spoke little Creole, he began to talk to them in broken English. François was a pleasant man, and he promised Mr. Christophe, "I am your driver. I will be taking care of you while you visit your family in Haiti. Welcome home, brotha!"

François had a great personality. It seemed as if he didn't have a care in the world. He and Mr. Christophe spoke about the politics of Haiti, and they chatted in Creole until they reached the Best Western hotel in Petionville. François unloaded Syd and Mr.

Chapter 12: Haiti

Christophe's luggage and assisted them in the hotel. Mr. Christophe tried to give François money, but he said, "Non, brotha à demain. Donne l'argent dans Cazale." Basically, he was telling Mr. Christophe to wait until tomorrow to give him money when he drives them to the village of Cazale. François smiled and said, "At what time, tomorrow morning, I pick you up?" Mr. Christophe answered, "See you here at ten o'clock." François graciously smiled again and wished them a great stay while in Haiti.

Syd and Mr. Christophe checked into their hotel but couldn't help but notice the security guards walking throughout the hotel with M16 assault rifles gripped in their hands. Mr. Christophe insisted that the security guards were hired by the hotel to protect the hotel's guests. Syd felt nervous yet relieved at knowing the armed security guards were there to protect tourists like herself. She also wondered out loud, "Why would the hotel need so many security guards? Did something happen in the past that required the hotel to employ security guards with M16 assault rifles?" "Stop worrying, Syd. Everything will be ok. We're here in

Haiti. We'll have a great time," Mr. Christophe confidently told Syd.

That afternoon, Syd and Mr. Christophe explored the hotel. Syd was pleasantly surprised that the hotel and spa were exactly as the online booking site had depicted it. The hotel, the spa, and the hotel room's décor were contemporary and clean. Syd and Mr. Christophe both were amazed that each staff member they encountered was friendly and provided excellent customer service. After checking out the hotel, Syd and Mr. Christophe headed to *Michele's*, the hotel's rooftop restaurant, for some authentic Haitian cuisine. Before they sat down for dinner, they enjoyed observing the art which adorned each wall. Syd had never seen such unique artforms in one place. Each piece of art was fabricated from thin pieces of metal. Each structure carried a deep story that resembled some sort of ancient spirit. If you gazed at the art long enough, the piece would reveal a captivating tale that only the imagination could handle. Syd and Mr. Christophe marveled at the creative pieces and tried to understand the deeper meaning behind each metal sculpture.

As they philosophized and compared thoughts about the exquisite art, a beautiful Haitian woman approached them. She asked, "Bonjour, will you be dining with us today? There's a table for you two outside near the bar." Syd looked at Mr. Christophe then answered the beautiful Haitian woman, "Yes, we are ready to have dinner. What do you recommend?" She smiled and said, "The *Griot, Legim, Pikliz,* and *Banen* are tasty." So, Syd ordered what the hostess recommended, but Mr. Christophe ordered the *Lambi* and *Legim*. Translation, Syd had pork, vegetables, and plantain, and Mr. Christophe had conch and vegetables. Syd enjoyed her first Haitian cuisine, while Mr. Christophe reminisced about how his meal reminded him of his mother's cooking. "My mother used to make *Lambi* on special occasions. This was one of my favorite dishes as a child. When I was growing up, I could smell the aroma of my mother preparing this dish while I was playing outside. Wow, Syd, this truly brings back old memories."

While they enjoyed the beautiful landscape of Haiti and finished their flavorful meals, the hostess brought two brown bottles of *Prestige* beer to their table. "While in Haiti, you must enjoy our beer," she kindly insisted that Syd and Mr. Christophe partake in Haiti's pride and joy. *Prestige* beer, which is manufactured in the Port au Prince, was a treat for Mr. Christophe. He proudly boasted that *Prestige* was his father's favorite beer, and he reminisced. "Each day, when my father finished work, he would always sit back and relax in his favorite chair, and this is the beer that he would have in his hands; *Prestige*." Syd listened to Mr. Christophe tell his story, and she knew that he was thrilled to be home.

HAITI DAY # 2

Early in the morning, François called the hotel to inform Mr. Christophe that he would arrive at one o'clock in the afternoon, instead of at ten o'clock in the morning to pick them up. He apologized for the inconvenience, and he also explained that he was having a minor issue with his vehicle. He communicated to Mr. Christophe that there would be a delay because he needed to have his vehicle repaired before traveling the

Chapter 12: Haiti

distance to Cazale. François explained, "There are no paved roads to enter the village. I don't know if we will make it. I must take my van to my friend; he is a mechanic. He will work on the van before I pick you up, and we should be ok." "No worries, man. We're on your time. Do what you need to do; we'll be at the hotel when you arrive," responded Mr. Christophe.

Mr. Christophe received another phone call; it was his cousin Philippe "Pep," from his father's side of the family. Pep enthusiastically told Mr. Christophe, "I'm on my way to the hotel. I'll be there in twenty minutes. I'll pick you up, so you can have breakfast with my mother. She doesn't know you're in town. It will be like a surprise."

As promised, Pep was at the hotel precisely twenty minutes later. He was elated to see his cousin, Mr. Christophe. He greeted his cousin with warm hugs and tons of questions. Syd and Mr. Christophe followed Pep to his SUV and conversed with him about his travels, family, and how excited his mother would be to see them. Within ten minutes, they arrived at Pep's home settled near the top of an affluent neighborhood in the

215

mountains of Petionville. Mr. Christophe said, "Wow, I didn't know that our hotel would be so close to where you live." In a scholarly French American accent, Pep replied, "Welcome, this is home."

Both Syd and Mr. Christophe were speechless before entering the securely gated brick mini mansion owned by Pep's mother. Astonished by the architecture of the home, they both just stared at how lovely the house was, then Syd said, "Wow, I can't believe something like this is in Haiti. I never imagined Haiti would have homes and neighborhoods like this." By the time they exited the SUV, Pep was locking the gate then opening the front door to his home.

Pep's mother, Gina, almost fainted when she saw Mr. Christophe walk toward her from the front door through the main foyer. She asked Pep, "Who is that? That's not Christophe. Oh my lord, Christophe! Look at you. You look the same, still handsome. And this must be Sydney! Christophe, is she Haitian? She's beautiful. You two make a good-looking couple. I'm so happy to see you! How long are you in Haiti? You must stay for breakfast."

Chapter 12: Haiti

Gina embraced them then ordered her three helpers to make enough breakfast for Syd and Mr. Christophe. As the helpers prepared homemade biscuits, fresh-squeezed orange juice, and scrambled eggs, Gina proudly showed Syd and Mr. Christophe family photos. She discussed every detail in the pictures concerning the people photographed and the year, date, and location that the photos were taken. Gina was sharp. She was an intelligent businesswoman, and you could see how much she loved her family. Her spirit was beautiful; her positive and vibrant energy filled every inch of her home. Although Syd was not related, Gina made Syd feel right at home. Syd was so impressed by the amount of love and affection given by Mr. Christophe's family. The visit to see Gina was a great way to start their vacation in Haiti.

Mr. Christophe told Pep and Gina about their travel plans while in Haiti. "Our driver François will meet us at the hotel this afternoon to take us to Cazale. I want to see the village where my mother was born and raised." "What time are you leaving? You must travel early; it's not safe to travel during the evening in Haiti, but if you leave early, you two will be fine," said Gina. "François had to work on his vehicle before taking us to Cazale. He said he would meet us at the hotel around one o'clock this afternoon," answered Mr. Christophe. "You two better get going, it's already twelve-thirty," Gina insisted that Pep hurry to take them back to the hotel. Gina graciously thanked Mr. Christophe and Syd for stopping by to visit. Tears of joy filled Gina's eyes as they departed and said their final good-byes.

    Pep dropped Syd and Mr. Christophe back at the Best Western hotel. They had enough time to freshen up, check out of the room, and settle the incidental charges acquired during their stay. Soon after closing out their tab and saying goodbye to the friendly hotel staff, François walked into the hotel and greeted Syd and Mr. Christophe with his same warm smile. "Bonsoir, now we go to Cazale," he said with excitement in his voice.

    The journey from Petionville to Cazale was like a bizarre rollercoaster. The driver, François, navigated through the congested non-regulated street traffic of Port au Prince, like a NASCAR race-driver. There were no stoplights, no minimum or maximum speed limit, and no governance to determine if the cars or pedestrians had the right of way. François was barely able to exit the city limits of Port au Prince without several drivers honking at his aggressive driving. "You are going to kill us driving like this," Syd said nervously while sitting in the backseat. François just smiled and kept on driving.

On the roads leading to Cabaret, which provides access to the village of Cazale, Syd took many photos of people utilizing Haiti's popular transit systems. The privately-owned *tap-taps* carried up to twenty people at a time, and mopeds that sometimes transported more than four passengers. Syd was fascinated to see women and children carrying baskets, filled with goods and wares, on top of their heads. She was amazed at the interrelated commerce, and entrepreneurial spirit of all the small-scale vendors that filled the streets. They were selling everything ranging from cooked meals, handcrafted art, and clothing items to vegetables, goats, and furniture.

When François arrived at the entrance of Cazale, he warned Syd and Mr. Christophe, "There is only one entrance into the village. The road is just rocks. It's not paved, so it will be very difficult to pass." "What happened to the road?" Mr. Christophe asked. "The road was damaged during the earthquake," François replied. François was accurate in his assessment of the road leading to Cazale. Without any success, he tried four times to drive through the rocky pathway. During his last attempt, Syd began to pray, "God, please help us pass through the rocks. We are in a remote part of the world; please help us get to our destination." God must have heard the prayer. Soon after, François slowly backed the van into reverse, then quickly shifted the gear into drive, and miraculously he was able to drive through the rocks.

As they finally made it up into the rural village of Cazale, there were very few visible signs of modern civilization. Many of the homes were built by hand, yet several modern homes were secured with tall brick walls and had solar panels. There were a few people that owned donkeys, and instead of carrying the baskets on their heads, the baskets were placed on the donkeys' backs to transport the goods. Syd witnessed a few people utilizing outdoor public water for showering and preparing their food. What stood out most was the abundance of school-aged children. As the children

Chapter 12: Haiti

walked the streets, in their uniform, they seemed to be very happy.

François drove on the dirt road of Cazale to safely get Syd and Mr. Christophe to the home where they would spend the next few days. When he approached their living quarters, he said, "Ok, this is your home for the next couple of days. There are no lights at night, so do everything before the sun goes down. The people of this village are all your family." François helped them with their suitcases and backpacks. When Mr. Christophe tried to give François money, François advised Mr. Christophe that he should give the money to his family instead. With keys in hand, François opened the door to Mr. Christophe's family home. The home was beautiful, just like Gina's home in Petionville. The only difference is that the house in Cazale had a massive wrap-around balcony and tile floors.

Syd and Mr. Christophe thanked François then he departed telling them, "You have my phone number, call me if you need to go into the city or call me if you need anything." They got familiar with their living arrangements, checked out all the rooms and decided that they would sleep upstairs in the bedrooms on the second level of the home. They both agreed that the balcony would be their hangout spot. They unpacked their bags, ate a few snacks, and relaxed on the comfortable balcony furniture until the sun went down.

    After the sun had disappeared, the main road of Cazale was extremely dark except for the occasional headlights of a moped driver transporting passengers throughout the village. If it weren't for the moonlight, there would've been no possible way to see anything. During the night, there were sounds of dogs barking and other animals making noise. Into the wee hours of the night, footsteps of people walking on the dirt road slowly faded away. Syd was concerned about her safety. She kept her eyes open the entire night. She wondered if the people in Cazale had noticed their arrival and if they did, were they ok with foreigners hanging out in their village.

HAITI DAY # 3

    Immediately before sunrise, the sounds of crowing roosters consistently howled to wake up the

Chapter 12: Haiti

village, and the sounds of footsteps pacing the dirt road began to increase. As Sydney sleeplessly laid in the bed, her daydreaming was pleasantly interrupted by the sounds of gentle knocking at the door. She got out of the bed and slowly walked down the stairs. When Syd got to the door and noticed there was no peephole, she nervously said, "Hello." The person on the opposite side of the door said in a distinctive Creole accent, "It's Essay. Je fais la petit déjeuner". Syd turned the dead-bolt lock to open the door so that she could let Essay in. After struggling with the menacing lock, Syd was finally able to prop the door open.

Essay stood at the door, bright-eyed and smiling, with two other Haitian women standing by her side. She told Syd, "My sistas et moi will prepare la cuisine. I will sleep here, but my sistas will stay only to help prepare your meals. Donnez-moi l'argent, give me money, and I buy everything to prepare your breakfast, your lunch, and your dinner." Syd smiled, embraced all three women, and trusted that Essay would handle everything concerning the kitchen. Syd excused herself to run up the stairs to get money for Essay. When she came back downstairs, she had money and her suitcase full of clothing items. Syd handed Essay fifty American dollars and asked, "Will this be enough for today?" Essay nodded her head, took the money, and handed all of it to her sisters, instructing them to purchase various food items. The sisters left the home, but Essay stayed and began to clean the kitchen. Syd asked, "What size clothes do you wear. I think I have some things that you might like." With a humble grin on her face, Essay innocently shrugged her shoulders because she didn't understand what Syd was talking about.

  Syd opened the suitcase and revealed each item of clothing to Essay, asking her, "Do you like this? I think you can fit this." Essay humbly nodded her head forward to indicate which articles of clothing she was interested in. She would roll her eyes and slowly shake her head from left to right when there was a clothing item that she didn't like. This went on for about an hour until half of the suitcase was empty. Syd was happy to give her gently used clothing to Essay because she knew that Essay greatly appreciated each item.

Chapter 12: Haiti

Mr. Christophe eased his way down the stairs and found Syd and Essay laughing and giggling about a weird clothing item that Syd had packed. Syd got up and introduced Essay to Mr. Christophe, "This is Essay, she will be staying here with us and preparing all of our meals." Mr. Christophe welcomed Essay and then asked Syd, "Can you please get dressed so we can visit my uncle at his church?" Syd replied, "Sure, we're just finishing up here. It won't take me long to get ready." Essay thanked Syd and went back to cleaning the kitchen. As Syd headed up the stairs, Essay warned her that the shower water would be cold and offered to prepare Syd a warm bucket of water for bathing. Syd had taken cold showers before, so she declined; she didn't want Essay to do any extra work to accommodate her. Syd was happy that Essay would be staying there to assist them with the meals.

After the brutally cold yet refreshing shower, Syd threw on her clothes and laced up her hiking shoes because she knew the adventure through the tropical forest in Cazale was about to begin. Syd headed downstairs and noticed that Essay's sisters had returned.

In admiration, Syd stood in the kitchen and watched the ladies work together in harmony. Within minutes they were placing several authentic breakfast dishes onto the table along with fresh-picked bananas and mangos pulled from the trees situated across from the home that they were staying in. After the ladies finished loading the table with food, Essay insisted that Mr. Christophe and Syd sit down to eat. "Mange, s'il vous plait," Essay said to them in an innocent voice.

While eating, Syd and Mr. Christophe couldn't help but compare the differences between Haitian food and American food. "Why do the eggs and toast taste so good?" Mr. Christophe asked. Essay informed them that the eggs came from the chicken, which lives outside in the back of the house. She said, "The eggs are fresh from the chicken this morning, and my sista makes the best bread in the village." Syd commented, "Even the bananas taste delicious. It's strange that the taste of the bananas would be so different than the ones back at home."

When Syd and Mr. Christophe completed their breakfast, they thanked Essay, and her sisters then exited the home. As they walked on the dirt road towards the church, Mr. Christophe pointed to a little handmade home. He said, "Syd, I'm not sure, but if I can remember correctly, I think that blue house, over there, is the home where my mother grew up." He and Syd continued to walk a little further until they arrived at the church owned by Mr. Christophe's family. The small chapel reminded Syd of the church she attended as a child. Mr. Christophe held out his hand to help Syd walk up the broken stairs, which lead to the entrance. They sat down in the back of the church to not disturb the morning mass. Aligned with several rows of small wooden benches; the church was packed to capacity with residents of the village.

    As Syd and Mr. Christophe tried to blend in with the congregation, it was evident that they were visitors to Cazale. When they entered the church and sat down, all the church members focused their attention on the foreigners. When Mr. Christophe's uncle, Jean, noticed them, a massive yet discreet smile was permanently plastered on his face. After the pastor completed the sermon, and the churchgoers took communion, the pastor switched from Creole to English and asked, "Do we have any visitors with us today?" After the prompts from the pastor, Syd and Mr. Christophe stood up in the back of the church. In front of the entire church, the pastor said to them, "Please come to the front of the church to introduce yourselves." Syd and Mr. Christophe did as they were told and walked up to the podium. Luckily for them, Uncle Jean stepped down from the choir and met them there. He took the microphone from the pastor and boldly told the church congregation, "C'est sont les enfant de mon soeur. Ils sont les enfants de mon maison." He was telling the people of Cazale that Mr. Christophe and Syd are the children of his home. He told the congregation that Mr. Christophe was the child of his sister.

When Mr. Christophe was handed the microphone, he nervously thanked his Uncle Jean then greeted the congregation in Creole. When Mr. Christophe started to speak in his native language, Syd was blown away. She had no clue that he was fluent in a second language because he never spoke anything other than English around her. Even while speaking with the

Chapter 12: Haiti

driver, François, and talking with Gina, Mr. Christophe communicated with them primarily in English. Syd listened in awe as Mr. Christophe so eloquently addressed the congregation with grace and sincerity. After giving his five-minute speech in Creole, Mr. Christophe handed the microphone to Syd. She reluctantly accepted the microphone, greeted the congregation, quickly introduced herself, then passed the microphone back to the pastor. Syd felt awkward standing in front of the church, speaking in English, so she immediately went back to her seat to sit down. Mr. Christophe remained at the front of the church, talking and catching up with his Uncle Jean.

    The pastor gave the benediction, and when the church was dismissed, all the church members made their way to welcome and hug Syd and Mr. Christophe. They both felt the warmth and love of the people of Cazale. Syd and Mr. Christophe followed Uncle Jean from the chapel to the porch of his home, which was the same house that Mr. Christophe had pointed to before arriving at the church. Uncle Jean proudly gave them a tour of his two-room home and explained to Mr.

Christophe that he was looking at the exact bed that Mr. Christophe's mother was born on. Uncle Jean also told stories about Mr. Christophe's father coming to that home, trying to court Mr. Christophe's mother when she was a young girl.

After touring the 100-year-old home, Uncle Jean took Mr. Christophe and Syd to his backyard then through a tropical forest to show them the family cemetery. While reading a list of names hand carved on the tomb, he sincerely explained in Creole, the history of each person buried within the above-ground gravesite. Syd listened, but she had no idea of what was being said. Out of respect for Uncle Jean and his family, she empathized and prayed to God. Syd was terrified of cemeteries. She didn't feel comfortable being at the gravesite. Still, she knew that it was important to Uncle Jean and Mr. Christophe.

Mr. Christophe listened intently as Uncle Jean continued to give facts about the family's history. Uncle Jean spoke about the massacre of 1969 and insisted that Mr. Christophe and Syd stay for the commemoration ceremony. Syd started to get worried as she thought

Chapter 12: Haiti

about celebrating the anniversary of a massacre. She wondered if the people who committed the killings would come back to the village to replay the devastating events from almost fifty years ago.

They left the family's gravesite and walked back through the lush tropical forest. They were engulfed in variations of greenery, farmland, and vegetation. Syd stayed close to Mr. Christophe as he followed Uncle Jean through the maze-like forest. Every time Syd looked up, she was introduced to a new tropical tree but couldn't resist from pulling a few low hanging fruit to munch on. Through leaves of the forest, Syd was able to notice several children playing in a body of water, so she said to Mr. Christophe, "Let's go check out the river. Look, it's over there." He told Uncle Jean that they wanted to see the river, so Uncle Jean pointed them to the easiest pathway to get there. He said to Mr. Christophe, "This land is yours and the river bleu over there it's yours too. I hold the deed to this land, and it belongs to the children of my sister." Mr. Christophe embraced and shook Uncle Jean's hand then he and Syd began to walk towards the river.

Not only were there children playing in the river, but they were also drinking the river water. It was amazing to see the Haitian women at the river collecting water in their huge containers then walking through the forest with the containers placed on top of their heads. Instead of being spectators, Syd and Mr. Christophe took their shoes off, dipped their feet in the water, scooped up water with their hands, and drank the refreshing blue water as well. Syd looked around, then glanced at Mr. Christophe and said, "When in Haiti, do as the Haitians. The taste of this water is amazing!" Mr. Christophe agreed, "Yes, the water is fresh. There must be a waterfall nearby."

After playing in the flowing river, Syd and Mr. Christophe walked through the forest. They eventually found their way back to the home. When they entered the house, Essay welcomed them and said, "I prepared lunch, but you go all day, so I prepared your dinner. S'il vous plait. Sit down. Mange!" Essay and her sisters had again prepared a fantastic meal. For dinner, they cooked goat meat, pikliz, banen, rice and peas. Essay also made

Chapter 12: Haiti

her specialty dessert and a homemade mixed drink that contained a generous amount of alcohol.

The food was so delicious that Syd and Mr. Christophe ate until they were completely full. They tried to help Essay clean the kitchen, but she wouldn't allow them to lift their plates. Essay took care of everything. Once Syd and Mr. Christophe finished their meal, many young children came to the back door where Essay would hand them the remainder of the food that she had prepared. Essay was a blessing to Syd and Mr. Christophe, but she was also a blessing to the people of Cazale.

Syd and Mr. Christophe retreated to their hangout spot on the balcony. While there, they enjoyed the evening ambience and a cool breeze. As nightfall began to approach, and the sun faded into the clouds, they conversed about Haiti until the village was completely dark.

HAITI DAY # 4

Around four o'clock in the morning, while there was no hope of daylight, Syd was awakened by the chants of what sounded like ancient African hymns. She could hear a group of voices outside singing rhythmic spiritual tunes. As the voices harmonized, each melody was strategically in sync as if the group had practiced and prepared the song for years. Syd had never experienced anything like this before, but she knew that it was some sort of sign from God. As the group of singers continued the hymn, Syd woke up Mr. Christophe and asked, "Can you hear that music? It's beautiful." Mr. Christophe said, "It sounds like a song my mother used to sing to me when I was a child. It's a Haitian hymn. They're just preparing for mass in the morning."

As the voices continued to harmonize, Syd went back to bed and thanked God for sending the angelic music, which provided a sense of peace and allowed Syd to rest well throughout the night.

Chapter 12: Haiti

Around seven o'clock in the morning, the dogs and roosters commenced their usual routine of barking and crowing, but Syd slept through the noise. She laid in bed while listening to Essay, and her sisters prepare breakfast. A few hours later, after inhaling the aroma of fresh bacon, Syd got out of bed, showered, threw on her clothes, then went downstairs for breakfast. She asked Essay, "Did you have to kill a pig to make the bacon?" Essay looked at Syd and tried her hardest not to laugh. She answered, "Yes, how else do you make bacon?" Syd probed and said, "But did you kill the pig with your hands?" Essay answered, "Yes my sista, what you do in America?" Syd explained, "We normally buy the bacon from the grocery store. It's packaged and processed before we take it home." "Everything here natural. We live off da land. When we cook, da meals are prepared with natural herbs and spices from da trees you see outside."

After Syd finished eating breakfast, she joined Mr. Christophe outside, and they began to stroll Cazale's main dirt road. Mr. Christophe asked, "Syd, what do you think about Haiti?" Syd paused for a moment, then answered, "It's different here. I can't believe how nice the people are. Why don't they tell us anything good about this place? They only report about poverty and corruption." "Could you see yourself living here on this island?" Mr. Christophe asked. "I don't know. Maybe. Actually, I was thinking about the children that came to the backdoor the other night to get food from Essay. I really want to do something to help them." "What would you like to do?" Mr. Christophe asked.

"I thought about possibly adopting a few of them, or maybe we can open a school here," Syd shared her deep thoughts with Mr. Christophe. He paused for a moment, then expressed his gratitude towards Syd, "This vacation has been more like a pilgrimage for me. I came here to visualize what life was like for my parents. I was able to see the home where my mother was born. I stood outside of the house and window, where my father regularly stood to court my mother. Syd, I've dreamed of the love my parents shared. I'm so happy to be here and experiencing Haiti with you. This has been the most important time of my life. I don't know why it's taken me this long to come back home, but I'm so glad to be

Chapter 12: Haiti

here with you." Mr. Christophe paused for a moment, took a deep breath, then turned to Syd and stared into her eyes. Syd knew how much the trip to Haiti meant to Mr. Christophe. She was impressed and fascinated by the history of the country. Still, more than anything, Syd admired the love and warmth that Mr. Christophe's family freely gave to both of them. She told Mr. Christophe, "It seems like your family accepts me as if I'm a part of their family too. They all seem so kind. Gina, Pep, Francois, Essay and the people of this village all seem to be genuinely happy. The children are chatty and vibrant. Seeing them dressed in their school uniforms and holding hands while walking to school each day really inspires me. There's a sense of community in this village that I've never experienced."

 Still staring into Syd's eyes, Mr. Christophe found the courage to say, "Syd, we have been friends for years, but I've wanted to be more than friends. I fell in love with you the moment I saw you at church. The first time I saw you, I knew that one day you would be my wife. I want to marry you Syd and spend the rest of my life with you. Syd stood there speechless as tears filled her big brown eyes then streamed down her cheeks. Mr. Christophe reached into his pocket, pulled out a small black velvet box, and handed it to Syd. Still crying tears of joy, Syd opened the box and screamed at the top of her lungs when she noticed the sparkling wedding band inside. Syd looked into Mr. Christophe's eyes and said to him, "You are a really good friend, and I've been thinking about us taking our friendship to the next level for many years. I just thought that if we stayed friends, we would always be together." Lost in the moment and captivated by the romance in the air, all the people in the village began to applaud and shout noises of what sounded like cheers of joy.

    A few minutes later, Mr. Christophe suggested to Syd, "Let's get married here, today in Cazale or at Bassin Bleu, with my family. We can have a small ceremony with the rest of our family and friends when we return to the States. Syd paused as she thought about Mr. Christophe's plans. She briefly reminisced about the pain from her past relationships; Syd had been scorned by love, so she was cautious about diving right into another serious relationship. As Mr. Christophe stared

Chapter 12: Haiti

into her eyes and waited for an answer, Syd gently asked Mr. Christophe, "Please allow me some time. I need to cleanse my heart and reconnect to my soul to God. Can you help me with something? Can you please take me to the river bleu? My Grandma Nadeya always instructed me to "wade in the water" when things were unclear, and I needed to hear from God. Grandma Nadeya said, "There's healing in the water." Mr. Christophe listened to Sydney's heart and he understood what Sydney was asking of him, so he held her hand and led her to the river bleu.

When Mr. Christophe and Syd arrived at the cobalt blue river, Syd instructed Mr. Christophe, "Please be patient with me. Stay right here. I must do this alone." Syd eased out of her sandals and began to walk slowly into the bleu. She looked up towards the sky with expectancy in her heart as she continued on the path to the center of the river. With each step the water welcomed Sydney's body. The current from the flowing bleu slowed down peacefully to receive and restore Sydney's soul. As she stood in the water, she prayed "Lord, you know what I have been through in relationships. This is a prayer for clarity. I believe that Christophe has demonstrated the kindness and love that I've longed for, but I want to be sure that this relationship is in your will, Lord. Please speak to me in such a way that I don't miss it. I need to hear from you, Lord. In your Son's name, Amen." Sydney paused for a moment in reverence; to take in the presence of God and fully understand the decision before her. As she turned back and headed to shore, she was hopeful that she would receive the confirmation she needed. She could see Christophe's gentle smile and hand out-reached to receive her. She glanced to her left and then to her right. Off in the distance on her right, she could see two other people in the water. A woman was being baptized. Sydney stopped in her tracks. She watched as the woman was submerged and lifted. Sydney looked towards heaven with a smile, reached out her hand towards Christophe and proceeded to the shore with a renewed perspective.

To Be Continued………

NOTE FROM THE EDITOR

Instant Classic!

Alicia's debut written work, Sydney's Bleu, grabs your heart. Whether you are single, married or divorced; male or female, young or older you will immediately have a vested interest in Sydney's journey. We all know someone like Sydney, who lives by the seat of their pants, loves hard, loves fast and loves fearlessly. This book not only brought back memories of my own search for love, it made me think about conversations to have with my children about love, and it strengthened my faith. Alicia's vulnerability and bravery shines through in this work. It was easy to see her heart, embrace her story and join her in this beautiful endeavor. I'm honored to be a part of Sydney's Bleu and I look forward to seeing what's next on her journey. Cheers!

Kelly Cook

ABOUT THE AUTHOR

Alicia Hilaire is the owner and operator of Suwanee Georgia's premier boutique spa and salon, Spa Li Cia. Alicia has an MBA from Georgia State University. Sydney's Bleu is her debut novel, which was conceived 20 years ago. Alicia is a francophone enthusiast and enjoys traveling to new and interesting cities around the world. She lives in Suwanee Georgia with her husband and children.

CPSIA information can be obtained
at www.ICGtesting.com
Printed in the USA
BVHW081932060220
571676BV00001B/2

9 780578 623962